SNOWBOARDING
Learning to Ride from All-Mountain to Park and Pipe

MOUNTAINEERS
OUTDOOR EXPERT
series

SNOWBOARDING
Learning to Ride from All-Mountain to Park and Pipe

Liam Gallagher

Foreword by Jesse Burtner

THE MOUNTAINEERS BOOKS

THE MOUNTAINEERS BOOKS
is the nonprofit publishing arm of The Mountaineers Club,
an organization founded in 1906 and dedicated to the exploration,
preservation, and enjoyment of outdoor and wilderness areas.

1001 SW Klickitat Way, Suite 201, Seattle, WA 98134

First edition, 2009

Distributed in the United Kingdom by Cordee, www.cordee.co.uk
Manufactured in the United States of America

Copy Editor: Christine Hosler
Cover and Book Design: The Mountaineers Books
Layout and Illustration: Heidi Baughman
Photographer: All photographs by the author unless otherwise noted.

Cover photograph: *Josh Dirksen, Canadian Mountain Holiday, Galena, British Columbia.* © Chris Wellhausen
Frontispiece: *When learning to ride, dwell not on how hard you fall, but how quickly you get up.*
Back cover photograph: *Blue skies and powder are what snowboarders live for.*

Library of Congress Cataloging-in-Publication Data
Gallagher, Liam, 1980-
  Snowboarding : learning to ride from all-mountain to park and pipe / by Liam Gallagher ; foreword by Jesse Burtner. — 1st ed.
      p. cm.
   ISBN 978-1-59485-265-7
   1. Snowboarding. I. Title.
   GV857.S57G35 2009
   796.939–dc22

                              2009019828

 Printed on recycled paper

Contents

Want to catch some air? Go build a jump. It's that easy.

Acknowledgments

Writing a book is kind of like snowboarding. It's an individual undertaking that's made a lot better when others are involved. I never thought I'd write a book before I turned 30. It's always been a goal of mine, but I've got a lot of "To-Do's" on the list and hammering out a 200-plus-page book wasn't exactly a priority just yet. Until, that is, I got an email from the folks at The Mountaineers Books. I'd like to thank Dana Youlin for deciding I was the man for the job. Everyone at The Mountaineers Books has been a pleasure to work with and I hope this book isn't the last I write for them. Thank you, Christine Hosler, for slogging through the first draft and making all those copy edits. Thank you, Mary Metz, for all your guidance and patience, even when deadlines were missed.

And to all the other snowboarders who contributed in some way to this book—thanks. Big thanks to Jesse Burtner for being a true ambassador for snowboarding. And thanks to photographer Chris Wellhausen for knowing how to nail a cover shot.

I owe my family the biggest thanks. Thanks, Pete and Mike, for being such cool brothers, friends, and real sources of inspiration. Thanks, Mom and Dad. If you hadn't let me escape to the mountains every weekend, I might never have ended up where I am today. Thank you for making so many sacrifices just so I could go play. I'm living my dream because of you.

And to all my friends, and anyone and everyone I've ever ridden with, thanks. Can't wait until we get to do it again. To the riders who risked limb and sometimes life for a photo, thank you. If you weren't out there putting it on the line, I'd be out of job and certainly a lot less inspired. So, thanks for snowboarding.

And, finally, thanks to anyone who has stood or aspires to stand on a snowboard. Thanks for trying and thanks for reading.

An empty pipe on a sunny day is the perfect place to learn the ropes of riding transition.

Foreword

Snowboarding ... where do I start? Let's just say that there isn't a day that goes by that I'm not thankful I'm a snowboarder. And there isn't a day that goes by when I'm not thinking about, watching, actively participating, or (in this case) writing about snowboarding. I've been a snowboarder for nineteen years now and it has challenged me, changed me, and ultimately made me who I am. It's been more than a sport, more than a hobby, more than a counterculture or another way down the hill; it has been nothing short of my entire life.

Snowboarding has acted as a lens, showing me the world like few things could. From the first time the bindings cinched down over my Sorels, I've experienced life as a mixture of fun, excitement, humor, and a bit of healthy fear with a snowboard as my vehicle. Obviously, I'm hooked on snowboarding. My board has instilled in me a deep-seated love of life, and I think that if you try snowboarding it will be the same for you.

The three hallmarks of the sport of snowboarding are friends, nature, and individual ex-pression. Through all my years as a snowboarder, it's these three basic things that keep the sport so interesting and progressive that I could never become bored with it.

People from all walks of life are brought together by the love of snow, adventure, and hilarity. The friends I've made over the years—from learning with school buddies in the backyard to competing on a global level with Scandinavian wunderkinds—make snowboard-ing what it is for me. We all push each other, help each other progress, and most important-ly, laugh at each other.

Being outside exercising is obviously an important part of snowboarding. But so often it's when you're between tricks or runs that you realize how lucky you are to be spending so much time outdoors. Whether you're in a city park or on a backcountry peak, time spent

Once you've experienced it for yourself, you'll understand why snowboarders love to lay into turns like this.

outside in reality—instead of inside, plugged into a virtual one—is time very well spent, good for the body, mind, and soul.

What originally drew me to snowboarding was the spirit of individualism it exuded. There's a sense of freedom and rebellion among snowboarders that includes you in the group while still letting you be yourself. A snowboard is an all-terrain vehicle; it can take you over anything, from mountain peaks, ponds, powder, ice, and trees to urban handrails, ledges, picnic tables, and hedges. A snowboard's range will stretch as far as its rider's creativity will take it, so it's a remarkable vehicle for self-expression.

I have yet to find a better way to connect with friends, nature, culture, and athleticism than the sport and lifestyle of snowboarding. I hope that you will find the inspiration within these pages to pick up a board and try snowboarding for yourself. Whether you hike the hill behind your school, hit a flat box in your backyard, or get the first chair on the gondola up Whistler Peak, you're about to discover the excitement, challenge, and accomplishment inherent in snowboarding. Come one, come all: it's better than the Hula-hoop and the pogo ball combined! It's new, it's different, and it's here to stay... it's snowboarding, and we want you!

Jesse Burtner, January 2009

Introduction

When I started snowboarding fifteen years ago, I had no idea it would take me as far as it has. Back then it was just something to do on the weekends. I'd been skiing for five years, but all my buddies were riding boards and it looked like a lot more fun. So I switched. I rented gear and went out on my own. My friends didn't want to wait for me, and I didn't want to hold them up. I wanted to catch up, so I rode as often as I could. I saved all my money for gear and lift tickets and dedicated all my free time to learning how to ride. It was a slow process and frustrating at times. I could fly down the hill on skis, but snowboarding proved to be an entirely different beast. Luckily, skiing had taught me how to use edges to stop, how to take a fall, and, most importantly, how to get right back up and keep at it.

I never took any lessons. I watched other riders closely and I taught myself.

And it wasn't long before I was riding right alongside my friends. They pushed me, and eventually I was pushing back. Together we all learned to ride and had a hell of time doing it.

Over the years, nothing's really changed. Snowboarding remains something that I really enjoy because of the friends I get to ride with. Shredding is an individual pursuit, but at the same time it's a shared experience and that much richer as a result.

Don't take my word for it. Find out for yourself. Save your money, buy some gear, look into lessons, find a crew to ride with, and get going.

I hope this book helps you along. Diving into any new pursuit can be intimidating, so I've tried to present all the information in a way that's easily digestible and accessible. The first chapter should give you a good idea about what you'll need to ride.

Sammy Luebke puts his Lib Tech Skate Banana to the test in Wyoming.

The second chapter provides a little history of snowboarding and introduces you to the fundamentals of riding. Chapters 3, 4, and 5 explore all-mountain, park, and pipe riding in more detail. All-mountain, which basically means resort riding, is the place every beginner should start. The park and the half-pipe are no place for newbies. Learn the fundamentals while riding the entire mountain and then move on to the park and the pipe.

After you experience all-mountain, park, and pipe riding the question will become not how you ride but what you ride. At that point ask yourself where you have felt most comfortable snowboarding. Or, better yet, what type of terrain was the most fun. If you find that one type of riding stands out as more fun than the others, then get to it and stick to it. Push yourself and progress your level of riding. Of course, your best bet might be to ride it all. Each type of riding teaches you something about the other types, so if you shred everything you'll become a well-rounded rider.

Once you've spent the season beating up your board, Chapter 6 will teach you how to repair all the damage you've done, while Chapter 7 should help you keep your body in shape so that you can ride longer and stronger.

Chapter 8 is about riding in the back-country because, once you feel really confident riding everywhere on the resort, you may want to start looking past the boundaries. Backcountry snowboarding is for intermediate and advanced riders; beginners shouldn't even consider exploring the mountains out of bounds. I hope Chapter 8 inspires you to approach this type of snowboarding with equal parts enthusiasm and caution.

Everything I know about snowboarding can be found in the following pages. My goal is to make your learning process easier. Every experience I've had while riding helped me write this book. And writing this book made me realize just how much I've learned along the way, both about how to get down the hill and about how to get through life. But you won't be hearing from just me in these pages. Tips from professional snowboarders are scattered throughout the text. You'll also find advice from experts on everything from choosing a line to surviving an avalanche in some longer sidebars.

Learning to snowboard can be a life-changing experience. Let it. It takes dedication. Don't expect the learning process to be easy, but remember: The things we have to work hardest for always yield the greatest rewards. I can honestly say I feel blessed to be a snowboarder. I hope you can say the same someday. I'm betting you will.

Good luck and have fun.

A NOTE ABOUT SAFETY

Safety is an important concern in all outdoor activities. No book can alert you to every hazard or anticipate the limitations of every reader. The descriptions of techniques and procedures in this book are intended to provide general information. This is not a complete text on snowboarding technique. Nothing substitutes for formal instruction, routine practice, and plenty of experience. When you follow any of the procedures described here, you assume responsibility for your own safety. Use this book as a general guide to further information. Under normal conditions, excursions into the backcountry require attention to traffic, road and trail conditions, weather, terrain, the capabilities of your party, and other factors. Keeping informed on current conditions and exercising common sense are the keys to a safe, enjoyable outing.

The Mountaineers Books

CHAPTER 1

Get ready to ride.

Gear

Decisions about gear should not be made in haste. There's a lot riding on those decisions—literally. Getting all the equipment you need to snowboard is no small investment. Simply put, snowboarding ain't cheap. The initial purchase of board, boots, bindings, outerwear, underlayers, and all the necessary accessories might be hard to justify if you're still not sure you're going to enjoy the act of sliding sideways on snow. All the gear, bought brand-new, will cost you about $1,000.

Nobody wants to drop that kind of money for products they haven't tested... which is why it's a good idea to rent gear when you're first getting into snowboarding. Try as many different products as you can before you buy. Do your homework, read gear reviews in magazines, and ask questions at your local snowboard shop. Figure out what works, what's comfortable, and what you're confident in, then buy accordingly.

If you buy the right gear, it should last you awhile. Sure, snowboarding equipment takes a beating, but better-built gear will withstand the abuse of any beginner or intermediate shred. A little extra money can go a long way when it comes to equipment, so don't cut corners. Buying used equipment is a great way to get what you need without breaking the bank, but the adage "you get what you pay for" certainly applies to snowboard equipment. When buying used equipment, spend time inspecting it for damage. Better yet, if you have buddies who know more about gear than you, get their opinion before buying. Snowboard shops often carry great used gear.

You need to trust that your equipment won't fail you. Having the right equipment can mean the difference between having a positive experience and having an off-putting experience on the hill. Understanding what you're looking for is the first step to a successful snowboarding career.

BOARDS

For the beginning snowboarder, the local snowboard shop can be overwhelming. With hundreds of boards to choose from, it's hard to know which one will work for you.

Know that most of these boards are more or less the same. There are subtle differences in size, shape, and flex, but the boards are pretty standardized. Most full-grown kids or adults ride boards that are cambered (curved upward along the edges), are almost symmetrical in shape, and are somewhere between 139 and 169 centimeters in length. However, for the first time in snowboarding's short history, snowboards are being produced in a variety of shapes. It's not uncommon for a rider to own one board built specifically for powder, one that's designed solely for park or pipe riding, and another that boasts of being an all-mountain board.

So how are you supposed to know which will suit your style of riding best? As a beginner, you shouldn't worry too much about which board to ride; all of them will feel more or less the same to you at first. As your skill level increases, you'll start to notice how different boards ride, but for now the most important thing is that the size (length and width) and flex are appropriate for your height and weight. Your local snowboard shop can help get you sized up and offer you a few options that'll work well.

You will want to consider what type of riding you'll do the most. Most any board will work for any conditions, but if you anticipate mostly doing one specific type of riding, then you can buy accordingly. Regardless of the type of riding you plan to do, expect to pay between $250 and $550 for your new board.

BOARD TYPES

All-Mountain Boards

If you're going to be riding the entire mountain, you want a board that'll handle it all. Honestly, any board will work, but some boards work better than others. Directional boards have traditionally been designed with the all-mountain rider in mind. They have long, wide noses and stiff tails. They're built with a directional flex pattern and have stances that are set slightly back. A board that can handle any type of snow, the directional board allows you to maneuver well and make quick turns.

An all-mountain board should be a little longer than a park board. You want to be able to ride this board in powder and in the trees, on groomers and in the park and pipe. Luckily, that's exactly the type of board snowboard manufacturers are building these days, so you shouldn't have any trouble finding one.

Boards for Park and Pipe Riding

Twin boards—so named because they're built with an identically shaped nose and tail—are best for park and pipe riding. The flex patterns on these boards are also symmetrical, and the stances are centered. This design allows the boards to be ridden equally well regular and switch. This is especially important for half-pipe, which involves a lot of switch riding. For park and pipe riding, it's best to use a shorter board with a centered stance and a medium flex.

Three boards with three different shapes. Numbered left to right: 1. This snowboard is a little longer and wider and would work well as an all-mountain board. 2. This board is a little shorter and has a twin shape, making it perfect for the park and pipe. 3. With its tapered shape and larger nose, this board is specifically designed to perform best in powder, but it can still be ridden in all other conditions.

Although most snowboards are similar in overall shape, the design of the noses and tails can vary greatly.

RIDING SWITCH

To ride switch is essentially to ride your snowboard backward. When you're riding switch, the foot that is typically your leading (or downhill) foot is your trailing or uphill foot. If you ride regular then your left foot normally leads; when you ride switch, your right foot becomes your leading, or downhill, foot.

Powder Boards

The number of specialized boards for sale is increasing every year, and most of the specialized shapes are designed for slashing powder. It seems to be a category that's here to stay. These boards come in a variety of shapes and sizes but share a few traits that make them float better in fresh snow. They are typically tapered, meaning the nose is wider than the tail. Powder boards run about 3 centimeters shorter in length than other types of snowboards. Their smaller size gives these boards a looser, more surfy feel.

SNOWBOARD TERMS

Learn the meaning of these terms before you go shopping for a board.

Length: The length of a snowboard from tip to tail; it will be measured in centimeters.

Effective edge: The section of a snowboard's edge that actually makes contact with the snow. A longer effective edge makes for a more stable and controlled carve, whereas a shorter effective edge makes for a looser board that turns more easily.

Sidecut (radius): This is the measurement of how deep the board's edges cut or swoop in from the nose or tail to the *waist*. A smaller radius makes for tighter turns, and a larger radius allows you to make longer, more arching turns.

Waist (width): The measurement of your snowboard at its narrowest point, in the middle. The width relates to the fit of your foot on the board. Generally, wide boards for larger feet start at 26 centimeters. Women's boards have narrower waists to accommodate smaller feet.

Toe edge: The stretch of your snowboard's edge that is under your toes.

Heel edge: The stretch of your snowboard's edge that is under your heels.

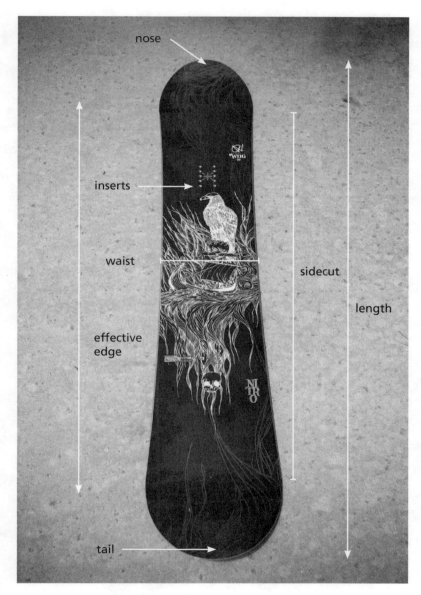

Anatomy of a snowboard

BANANA TECHNOLOGY EXPLAINED BY PETE SAARI

Mervin Manufacturing, makers of Lib Tech and Gnu Snowboards, sparked a design revolution when they released their new line of Banana Technology boards in 2008. Snowboards have always been built with *camber*, like skis, but the guys at Mervin decided one day that snowboards would be more fun if they had *rocker*, like surfboards. So they designed, built, and tested boards that were shaped kind of like bananas, that is, curved up at both ends. They found that these boards do in fact work really well. Now many companies are latching onto this new shape; it's proving to be a design that's here for good. This is an interview with Pete Saari, co-founder of Mervin, who's been building snowboards since the early 1980s.

Liam: Explain Banana Technology.

Pete: Banana Technology is Lib Tech's new snowboard technology, designed around the needs of a snowboarder. Traditional snowboard design borrowed camber from skiing in order to make snowboards work better on hardpack. Camber is designed to work well with one central pressure input area (i.e., boot) on each ski, but it was not really designed for how a snowboarder uses a board. Camber leaves an unweightable "dead zone" between your feet. Banana Technology focuses edge pressure between your feet, bringing the dead zone to life. It adds catch-free tips and tails for jibs, rails, and forgiving landings. It adds pre-bent rocker between your feet for edge hold and carving, and it adds tip and tail float in powder.

Liam: How did you guys think this up?

Pete: Lib Tech is an R&D [research and development] company. Mike Olson and our ExperiMental crew designed our entire shop and all our tooling around change and evolution. We have been experimenting every year all year for over twenty-five years and still were not completely satisfied with snowboard designs. They still kind of sucked compared to surfboards, skateboards, and skis. It finally came to us—camber is for skiers. Snowboarders need a board designed around snowboarding. Banana Tech is designed for snowboarders. I can't believe it took us so damn long to figure it out. Banana Tech is what a snowboard was always supposed to be.

Liam: What kind of testing did you have to do before you were confident it worked?

Pete: We were confident Banana Technology would be the future even before we rode it. We have been thinking about snowboard geometry every day for years, so once we had Banana Tech in our heads, we pretty much knew it was a go. The actual testing was almost a formality, but it sure was fun to see all our theories actually working. It's great to know that Banana Tech is letting riders push snowboarding to new levels everywhere from backyard jibs, everyday park shredding, to Torah Bright winning the icy pipe at the U.S. Open and people doing gnarly big mountain Alaskan lines. Basically we work on snowboards every day and it sure is nice to build and ride boards that make you work less, ride better, and put a big smile on your face.

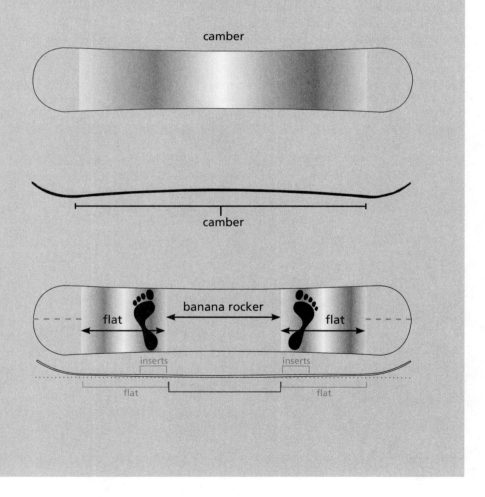

BOOTS

Snowboard boots have come a long way. It wasn't too long ago that shreds only had two choices: Kamiks or Sorels. It was definitely a lesser-of-two-evils scenario back then. Fast forward twenty years. Snowboarders are now faced with all kinds of options when choosing their boots. There are boots designed especially for park riding and others built for backcountry exploits. There are heat-moldable liners, liners that promise to stymie the stink, and liners that allow you to comfortably squeeze into a boot that's a half-size smaller. But despite all the advances in technology, when you're choosing a boot, one criteria still takes precedence: the fit. Even with the best board and bindings, a pair of boots that fits poorly can ruin your snow-sliding experience.

FINDING THE RIGHT FIT

You're bound to be in these boots for countless hours, so you should make your choice carefully. Your feet will thank you. And your riding will be better in a boot that fits

With all the snowboard boots available these days every rider should be able to find a pair that fits like a glove.

like a glove. If your boots are too loose, you're liable to turn an ankle. But end up in boots that are overly constricting and your feet will fall asleep. Eventually you'll feel as if you've been fitted with a pair of concrete slippers. Then you're sunk.

When it comes to finding boots that fit, it's a fine line between too loose and too tight. With patience and careful attention, you can find just the right fit and ensure your boots fit well, perform like they're supposed to, and keep your feet warm first chair to last.

The best way to figure out which boot is right for you is to go into your local snowboard shop and try on as many pairs as you can. Wear the socks you plan on riding in, and take a bunch of different boots for a test drive. Walk around the shop, jump around, bend your knees, test the flex, and feel for pressure points or any other areas of discomfort. Even the smallest pinches are sure to aggravate you as the season wears on. Ask if you can strap into a pair of bindings—preferably the same ones you ride in—so you can get an idea about how the boots will fit into those bindings.

Testing boots at the shop might not seem like an effective way to judge the fit, but you'd be surprised how much you can learn by simply lacing them up and walking around for a few minutes. Odds are if they feel good right off the bat, you've got a pair of boots that'll keep your feet happy all winter long.

CHOOSING A BOOT STYLE

Expect to spend between $100 and $250 for a pair of boots. Boots come in a variety of flexes, with softer boots for those looking for more comfort than performance and stiffer flexes for snowboarders who want really responsive boots. When you're just getting started, a softer boot will do; you should be more concerned with keeping your feet happy than with wearing a stiffer boot that's made for more advanced riders. A more forgiving boot that's flexible and fits well will do you just fine for your first couple of seasons of snowboarding. Then, as you become more skilled, start looking for more performance in your boots.

LACING SYSTEMS

Today's snowboard boot cobblers offer so many different lacing systems that it's hard to know which one's right for you. Remember, regardless of how the boots lace up, what's most important is how your foot fits inside. While some lacing systems might seem faster, easier, or more attractive for one reason or another, if the boot doesn't fit, there's no lacing technology that can help. See the following pages for today's lacing systems.

Traditional bow and loops laces. This is the lacing system that all of us grew up with. The most obvious drawback is that the old-fashioned system takes longer to lace up than the newer systems. But it's a time-tested design that allows you to lace your boots exactly the way you prefer. You can't go wrong with boots that you lace up. You already know how to operate them, and if the laces break—which they will—you'll be able to pick up a new pair of laces at your local snowboard shop.

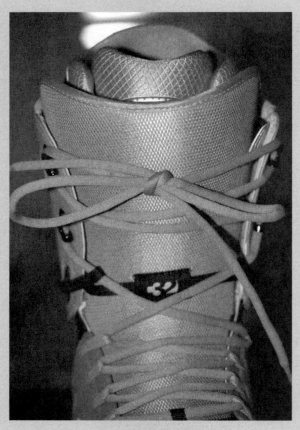

You can't beat an old-fashioned pair of laces.

Speed-lacing systems. A lot of companies now make boots with speed laces. Different areas of these boots can be tightened with the pull of a cord, which allows for a custom fit all over your foot. The drawback is that if the pull-cord breaks, you'll have to get creative about how to keep your boot tight. While speed-lacing systems might make tightening your boots easier and quicker, they're typically more expensive and it's doubtful that you will notice much of a difference in performance.

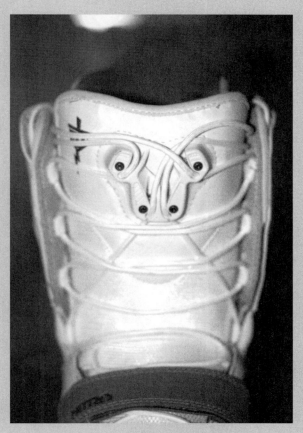

*One of many speed-lacing systems offered by snow-
board boot makers*

Boa. Often extolled as the fastest and most convenient lacing system on the market, the Boa lacing system replaces laces with wire and is arguably the most high-tech offering to date. You tighten your boots with a turn of the dial and release the wire with the punch of a button. It's a simple system, but you're putting a lot of trust in a wire that can—and does—break. Another drawback is that Boa boots tighten uniformly across your foot, so you aren't able to tighten certain sections while leaving others more loose.

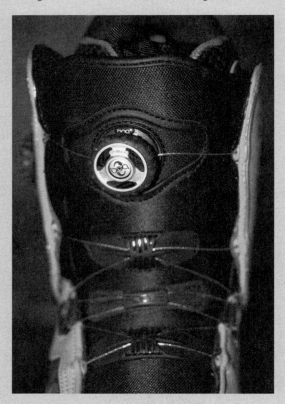

This boot is equipped with two separate Boa dials so it can be custom fit to any foot.

FITTING YOUR BOOTS

Of all the equipment that snowboarders struggle with, boots require the most tweaking, fine-tuning, and fiddling. If you want a softer, more flexible feeling that allows for a lot of movement in your ankles, leave your boot a little looser around the top. Be sure to keep your laces tight around your ankles, because you never want to allow much play in that part of your boot. Loose ankles are prone to twist, so if you find that your boots loosen themselves throughout the day, take the time to stop and re-tie them. A minute spent tending to your boots could save you months of downtime due to an injury.

Keep in mind that over a season your boots will *pack out*, that is, the foam in the liners will compact and you'll end up with more wiggle room. You might have to pull the boots tighter later in the winter as the liners become less bulky and subsequently less supportive.

If you find that your toes get bitter cold, numb, or occasionally turn blue, your boots are most likely tied too tight around the lower foot. This is the best way to ruin a day. Once you lose circulation to your feet, you'll experience a lot of discomfort and your riding will suffer—not to mention the possibility of frostbite if you ignore your frozen toes all day. Keep your laces a little looser if you find this happening to you. And don't hesitate to take your boots off during lunch to really let the blood start flowing again.

> "I always do the wrap-around-the-back technique and tie the laces in the front. Wrapping the laces around the top of the boot just gives you a little more support."
>
> *Erik Leines*

CARING FOR YOUR BOOTS

Proper care of snowboard boots is another oft-overlooked topic. No other piece of equipment takes as much abuse as your boots, so your level of care should increase accordingly. Dry your boots after every day on the hill. Remove the liners and let them air-dry overnight. Or buy a boot dryer and put your boots on there as soon as you peel them off your feet. And don't wear your boots when you don't have to. Any unnecessary time in those things will cut into their lifespan. Don't put on your boots for the drive up to the mountain. Your feet will sweat, and that sweat will cool and make your feet cold once you're on the hill.

BINDINGS

Bindings are the direct link to your board. A good pair of bindings should feel as if they're not even there. It's essential that your bindings fit your boots properly. They're typically made in three sizes: small, medium, and large. Small bindings will fit

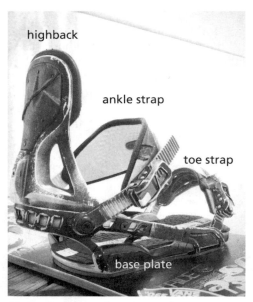

highback

ankle strap

toe strap

base plate

Bindings are your direct connection to your board so make sure you get a pair that fits your boots well.

men's boot sizes 5–7, mediums will work with sizes 8–10, and those of you wearing boots size 11 and up should look for a pair of large bindings. Other bindings are built for kids and women. It should be obvious what size bindings you'll need, but if you're feeling clueless, ask the employees at your local snowboard shop to match your boots to the right bindings.

Every pair of bindings is designed with an almost infinite number of micro-adjustments so you can custom-fit them to your boots. No bindings feel like they fit perfectly in the shop—you'll probably have to make adjustments to them later at home.

Pay attention to the number of moving parts on any pair of bindings you consider buying. Bindings see a lot of use, and more movable parts equates to more parts that might break. Don't hesitate to ask what the bindings are made of before you buy. Most bindings are made of either plastic or aluminum. Plastic bindings are typically a little more flexible, while aluminum ones feel a little stiffer. Both types perform basically the same. As with any piece of snowboard equipment, spending a little extra money for a product made of better materials will usually get you a binding that will last longer. Expect to spend between $120 to $250 for bindings.

TYPES OF BINDINGS

Never before have there been so many ways to keep your snowboard underfoot. While all these options are exciting for more advanced snowboarders, beginners can find it hard to discern what the differences are and, more importantly, how these differences will affect how they ride. Three types of bindings are currently on the market. Here's a breakdown of what each style has to offer.

Industry Standard

This could be considered the old standby. Undoubtedly most snowboarders have ridden with standard bindings for the majority of their snowboarding lives. While this binding type has been around a long time, manufacturers continue to improve on the design.

This design consists of a base plate, a

With all the subtle differences in bindings these days, it can be tough to know which pair is best for you. Remember, fit should be your first priority.

highback, and two straps. Highback design has come a long way, but the highback is still there essentially to make your binding respond when you need it to. Taller highbacks provide more support and make your board respond more quickly, but they can also put added strain on the calves and cause unnecessary pain for the beginning snowboarder. You want a highback that isn't too tall (meaning it rises too high on your calf and puts too much pressure on your leg) or too stiff (one that doesn't have enough flex for your level of riding and subsequently feels uncomfortable). The softer

the flex of the highback, the more forgiving it'll be. When you're learning to ride and adjusting to the feeling of bindings, you want all the forgiveness you can get.

Speed-Entry
In 1996, Flow released the first reclining-highback bindings, and the company continues to make these flagship speed-entry bindings. These days, more and more bindings are being built with speed in mind. We all want to ride more, and the strap-in process is an obvious place to cut back on wasted time. With reclining highback

bindings, you leave your straps adjusted the way you like them and simply kick your foot in and out of the binding by flipping the highback up or down. The advantage is that you spend less time strapping in. When you're learning to ride, you spend a lot of time strapping in and undoing your bindings, so speed-entry bindings can save you a lot of bending over or sitting down in the snow.

These bindings don't perform any differently than standard binders; they just make the strap-in process a little easier for the beginner. Rental shops typically stock some of these bindings, and the best way to determine if they're right for you is to test them out. Try speed-entry bindings for a day, see what you think, and then make your decision.

EST

Burton, always a company pushing the boundaries of equipment design, in 2006 introduced its new EST line of bindings, one of the most notable new designs in recent snowboard history.

EST stands for "extra sensory technology," which is a fancy way of saying these bindings allow you to feel your board better. Burton replaced the rigid base plate of standard bindings with foam to heighten board feel. These bindings are softer to stand on and allow for a truer flex in your board.

EST bindings are specifically designed for Burton boards built with ICS (infinite channel system), so if you want to try these bindings, you'll have to try a Burton ICS board, too. Again, the rental shop at your local mountain should have some you can try before you buy.

Odds are the beginning rider doesn't really need all this added feel and flex. You'll probably be busy enough just getting used to how your bindings respond. But Burton bindings have long since been the Cadillacs of snowboard bindings, so it's safe to say you can't go wrong with the EST.

CLOTHING

Snowboard clothing has come a long way from the early days of jeans and flannel. Today, every snowboard brand offers functional outerwear and underlayers.

OUTERWEAR

Quality outerwear is essential. A day spent snowboarding is a day spent braving the elements. You will get cold and wet and want to retreat to the lodge. Wear the right outerwear and you'll be able to last that much longer out on the hill. And ultimately, the more time you spend on the snow, the better rider you'll become.

What you need most is outerwear that's both waterproof and breathable. Most of today's snowboard outerwear is ranked on how waterproof it is. You can find this ranking clearly marked on the jacket or pants. The rating system starts at 5000 mm and goes up to 30,000 mm. Unless you're riding in some seriously soggy conditions, a waterproof rating around 10,000 mm should do the job.

It's equally important to pay attention

to outerwear's breathability rating. If your outerwear isn't breathable, all the moisture emanating from your body will be trapped inside the jacket. That moisture will cool, making you cold and quickly ruining your day on the hill.

As with any snowboard equipment, price is proportionate to quality. Better outerwear costs more. You can expect to spend between $150 and $300 for a good snowboard jacket and a little less for pants. Before you buy, consider how much you'll use your outerwear. If you expect to snowboard every weekend all winter, it will be worth your money to spend a little more on high-quality outerwear. On the other hand, if you imagine you'll only go up to the hill a handful of times, then you can get away with less-expensive gear.

If you're torn between spending more of your hard-earned money on pants or a jacket, consider this: You will spend a majority of your time on your butt. A good pair of pants can make your learning experience a lot more pleasant. Invest in durable, water-resistant pants and you'll keep your lower half a lot drier. If you're going to spend a little more, spend it on the pants.

UNDERLAYERS

Layering is a more effective way to stay warm than simply relying on a big, bulky jacket. It's easy to dismiss the benefits of underlayers and resort to a t-shirt and hooded sweatshirt, but spend even one day on the mountain with cotton as your first layer and you're bound to be miserable by last chair … assuming you even last that long. With all the advancements in fabrics these days, it's foolish not to employ technology to keep yourself warm.

A long-sleeve capilene shirt serves as a great first layer. This fabric wicks moisture away from your skin, keeping you warm and dry. These shirts are generally pretty thin, so you'll want another layer to put on top of it.

Mid-weight fleece is always a good choice for a second layer. It's a bit thicker and heavier, providing a lot of insulation. These two layers—the capilene shirt plus the fleece—underneath a jacket should keep you warm in temperatures as low as 15 degrees Fahrenheit. If the mercury dips much lower, you'll probably want to consider another outer-underlayer.

Underlayers with hoods work well for snowboarding because they provide a little extra protection around your neck, and you can pull them up tight around your head if the weather really moves in. Pay attention to the length of your underlayers. Shirts that are too short for your torso can come untucked, creating a lot of discomfort and letting in snow when you take the inevitable fall.

Socks are an oft-overlooked part of your snowboard outfit. Your feet take a lot of abuse while riding, and a good pair of socks can make a world of difference. Avoid cotton socks at all costs. When your feet sweat, cotton will get wet, cool, and freeze your feet. Synthetic or wool socks are best. Avoid socks that are too bulky; they're liable to be too thick to be comfortable. Also, make sure your socks come above the top of your boots. Knee-high socks are always a good call. Your feet need a little breathing room, so don't layer your socks. One pair of good socks should do.

Some socks are specifically designed for snowboarders, with sections of padding and thinner material where snowboarders need it. Your local snowboard shop should stock a bunch of them.

If you continue to get cold feet, you probably need to head to the lodge, peel those boots off, and let your dogs warm up for a minute. Don't fret—it happens to the best of us.

ACCESSORIES

A few additional purchases can make your snowboarding experience safer and more enjoyable.

HELMETS

Helmets are gaining a lot of popularity in snowboarding, and for good reason. It's easy to hit your head while riding. But wait, snow is soft and forgiving, right? Why would I need to wear a helmet? With the presence of so many unforgiving surfaces—ice, trees, rails, lift towers, etc.—and the speed at which you move when snowboarding, head injuries are a very real threat. Since today's lightweight designs and levels of comfort and warmth rival a beanie, wearing a helmet is pretty much a no-brainer. Basically, if you value your brain and want to push yourself to snowboard more aggressively, wear a hel-

met. Snowboard helmets cost between $60 and $120.

GOGGLES

Goggles come in all shapes, sizes, and prices. As far as gear goes, a good pair of goggles is priceless. If you're snowboarding anywhere with any kind of winter weather—which is pretty much everywhere—you need goggles. Try making a run without them in a snowstorm.

It's miserable. And dangerous. With all the different goggles on the shelves these days, it can be hard to know exactly what you're looking for... or, rather, through.

It's most important to buy a pair of goggles that fits your face. Make sure there are no gaps where air or snow could get in. Goggles should feel snug and more or less sealed against your face. A good pair of goggles feels as if you're not even wearing them. Choose the right fit over any fancy features. There isn't a lot of difference between a $50 pair of goggles and a $150 pair. The more expensive ones probably won't fog up as easily, but both will offer about the same level of eye protection.

One thing to consider when buying goggles is the tint of the lenses. You want to buy a pair that is tinted appropriately for the conditions you ride in most often. If it's usually foggy with low light, look for a pair with yellow or orange lenses. If it's always sunny and bright, buy goggles with darker tinted lenses, maybe even mirrored lenses. Again, the employees at your local snowboard shop will be a great resource when it comes to choosing your goggles.

FACE MASKS

Windburn and frostbite are some of the nasty side effects of snowboarding. Some days you just have to cover your face. All kinds of face masks are specifically designed for snowboarding these days. These specialty masks are both functional and fashionable. Designed with air holes around the mouth and different thicknesses of fleece or wool, most of today's face masks are incredibly comfortable and cozy. When buying a face mask, look for one that's snug but doesn't feel like it's suffocating you. You breathe heavily when you snowboard, so make sure the fabric isn't so thick that it inhibits exhalation. Expect to spend anywhere from $15 to $40 for a high-performance face mask. Or, if times are tough, pick up a bandana for a buck or two.

PREPARING YOUR EQUIPMENT

Now that you've spent a couple of months' rent on all that equipment, you need to take some steps to ensure it all rides like it should. If you buy your board and bindings together at the same shop, you can probably ask the staff to set up the bindings for you, but keep in mind that mounting bindings is something every snowboarder needs to know how to do. You should be comfortable standing strapped into your board before you head up to the hill. Take some time to learn how to not only mount but also adjust your bindings. Get them set up in what seems like the best way for you, and your first day on the hill is sure to be that much better.

MOUNTING YOUR BINDINGS

As important as it is to get the right board and bindings, it's equally important that your binders are mounted to your board correctly. You only need two, three, or four bolts to attach them to your board, depending on the brand of the bindings. Take the time to do this correctly. Properly mounting your binders will ensure that your board performs like it should, you can slash safely, and, most importantly, you can feel entirely confident doing so.

Preparing to Mount Your Bindings

When you buy a fresh pair of binders, they come with all the hardware needed to mount them on your board. You need one bolt for every insert (hole in the top of your snowboard). With three- and four-hole pattern boards, you might get away with using fewer bolts than the board requires, but don't try it. Your bindings won't be tight enough, so in time they'll loosen and start to wiggle, and they might twist at the worst possible time.

Once you have your bindings out and ready to mount, make sure you're working with a number-three Phillips-head screwdriver. It's the tool that will best fit your hardware. Using the right screwdriver will prevent you from stripping those bolts and allow you to tighten them sufficiently.

Although the ergonomic design of most of today's binders makes it pretty obvious which one goes where, every snowboarder has managed to mount the right binding where the left one goes and vice versa. The key is to identify which binding fits which foot and mount accordingly. Keep in mind that your binding ratchets will always be on the outside of your foot.

"Once I get my bindings on, I always take a permanent marker and trace around them on the top sheet of my board. That way, when I switch to my other boards or just happen to take off my bindings, I can throw them back on without measuring out my stance."

Eddie Wall

Determining Stance

Before you can mount your bindings, you need to figure out your stance. Many snowboarders set up their boards with a stance that's all wrong for them. Too narrow of a stance and you're liable to topple like a toddler. Too wide and you won't be able to turn your board properly. Today's bindings offer an almost infinite number of stance options, so there's no reason for your board to be set up with the wrong stance.

The first thing to figure out is whether you ride regular, with your left foot leading, or goofy, with your right foot in front. There are many theories about how to determine which way you ride. Some suggest that you run and slide across ice or a slick floor in socks and see which foot you automatically lead with. Others suggest having someone push you when you're not expecting it, to see which foot you extend to brace yourself. Whichever foot goes out is the one that you'll lead with when snowboarding. Again, your local shop is a great place to get advice. Or better yet, head up to the hill; try riding regular for a day, then goofy the next, and see which feels more natural.

Either way, it's important to pick a stance and stick with it when you're learning to ride. Consistently riding either regular or goofy will make the learning process much quicker. After you've figured out which way you want to ride, you can mount your bindings accordingly. If you're regular, plan to mount your left binding on the inserts that are closest to the nose and your right one on the inserts closer to the tail; vice versa if you're goofy.

Once you've figured out whether you're riding regular or goofy, take some time to dial in your stance width. Stance width is the distance between the centers of the two bindings, or simply put, how far apart your feet are on the board. As a general rule, you want your snowboard stance to be a little wider than the width of your shoulders. Snowboarding is done almost entirely with your lower body, so you want to find the stance that allows the widest range of motion.

It's important to dial in your stance width and binding angles with your boots on, because your boots require different posture than street shoes. To get a feeling for how the boots will ride on a hill, lace them up tight, strap in, and wiggle around a bunch.

Put your board, sans binders, in front of you. Stand with your feet a little wider than shoulder width. Do a few squats and jumps, each time putting your feet a little closer together or wider apart. Notice how your stability changes. You want to mount your bindings at the width that feels most comfortable and most stable.

Once you get your stance figured out, take a tape measure and make a note of exactly how wide it is, so that you've got a point of reference for the next board you set up.

Now that you've determined how far apart your bindings should be on your board, you are ready to bolt the base plates of your bindings into the inserts (holes) in your snowboard. One by one, insert each bolt into the hole and tighten it halfway. With the binders in place, stand in them with your boots on, to figure out if the stance width and stance angles feel natural.

Stance angles are the angles at which your bindings are situated on your board. On your bindings you will find little notches in the base plate with numbers corresponding to the angles. Stance angles are all about personal preference. Some riders like a lot of angle, while others prefer hardly any angle. Good angles for beginners to try are positive 15° to 20° on the front foot and negative 10° to 15° on the back foot.

Try jumping in the air again; when you land, notice the angle of your feet to your body and to each other, then take these angles and set up your bindings similarly.

Later, after you've moved past the beginner stages of snowboarding, you can start exploring different stance options. Certain types of riding or terrain can be easier to ride with a different stance width. If you're going to be lapping the park at the local hill, a little wider stance will probably suit you best. More width usually makes it easier to spin when you jump. It also requires your body position to be more of a squat, which lowers your center of gravity and helps you tackle freestyle riding that focuses on tricks.

If it's deep powder snow you plan on charging, set up your stance a little narrower. A narrower stance makes it easier to turn your board quickly and gives you the response time needed for maneuvering around trees, steeps, or any other obstacles the mountain might throw at you.

Finally, it's always good to pay attention to riders who are similar in stature to you and see how wide their stances are. That can help you get an idea about what stance width might work best for you.

Tightening the Bolts

When tightening your bolts, don't crank one down all the way before moving on to the next. Instead, half-tighten each one, then work your way back around, tightening each a little more until they're all good and snug. This will ensure equal amounts of pressure on all the contact points of your base plate.

No matter how tight you get your bolts, they will loosen up on their own as you use your board. Always check your hardware before you ride and also throughout the day. Every resort should have a tuning bench in the base area, with a screwdriver that you can use to make any additional adjustments. Make it a habit to batten everything down before you head up the hill. If you don't, you might end up losing a screw out there. That's why it's a good idea to always carry a couple extra bolts in your pocket. You never know when you might need to replace one that mysteriously goes missing—or to offer one to a fellow snowboarder in need. Your local snowboard shop or the resort's rental shop should have buckets of extra bolts. Don't hesitate to ask if you can buy a couple.

ADJUSTING YOUR BINDINGS

An almost infinite number of micro-adjustments can be made to custom-fit your bindings to your boots. This process of tweaking your toe and ankle straps and highbacks should not be overlooked. The fit of your bindings can have a profound effect on how you ride.

Once you begin riding, you'll find that your binding straps, like a lot of other snowboard gear, need a little adjusting every now and again. There are many reasons to make minor adjustments: Maybe your boots are packed out, or your ankles are swollen, or you're just looking for a little more give or perhaps more response. Whatever the reason, don't hesitate to fine-tune your bindings.

Since the bolts on your straps vary in size, you need screwdrivers with small heads. Get a range of sizes of Phillips screwdrivers, or consider buying a snowboard-specific tool. These little tools are easy to carry with you on the mountain and are sure to have all the bits and pieces you need to keep your bindings tuned up.

The ankle straps on your bindings are designed to hold your feet in place comfortably. If comfort is the last word that comes to mind when you think of your ankle strap, look at the length of the strap. Make sure the strap is centered between one side of the binder and the other—that is, that it isn't too long or too short for your boots. If the strap is too long you won't get a snug enough fit, but if it's too short you'll put unnecessary strain on the *ladder* (the plastic strap that attaches to your toe or ankle strap) and it'll be a noticeably awkward fit. The employees at your local snowboard shop should be experts at adjusting straps, so never hesitate to ask them to help. It's what they're paid to do.

Besides adjusting the length of your ankle straps, you should be able to change where the straps attach to your bindings. Tweaking exactly where the straps span your feet has a significant impact. Mounting your straps in the higher holes gives you more support and makes your bindings more responsive; attaching them lower down on the heel cup gives you more flexibility and a looser feeling.

Not much adjusting can be done to toe

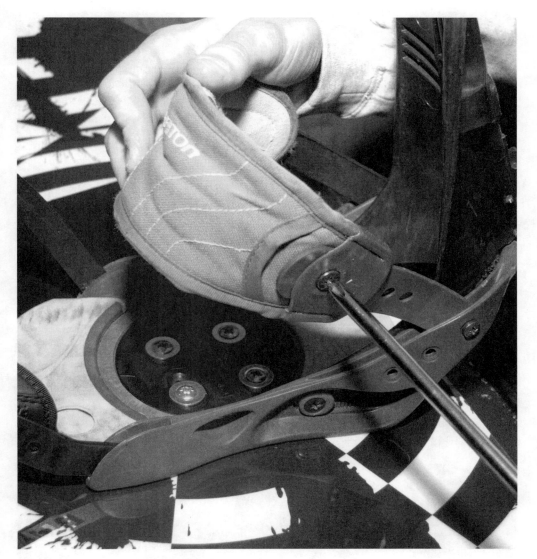

Most ankle straps are adjustable with the turn of just one screw.

Toe straps can be adjusted with a Phillips screwdriver.

To adjust the forward lean of your bindings, look for the small device that slides up and down on the back of the highback.

straps. These days most toe straps could be classified as cap straps, because they wrap around the toe of your boot, rather than across the top of your foot. Whatever the style of your toe straps, make sure the length of each strap allows it to easily conform to the contour of your boot.

Besides adjusting your ankle straps and toe straps, you can give yourself more or less forward lean by tweaking the highbacks on your binders. Forward lean (the degree to which highbacks are angled forward) can be your best friend or your worst enemy. When properly employed, forward lean allows you to use your heel edge in ways you never thought possible. On the other hand, forward lean utilized incorrectly can severely stifle your shredding. It's a fine line.

Simply put: Forward lean keeps you on your toes. It makes you bend your knees more, so even a little puts you in that "ready" position. Forward lean increases responsiveness in your bindings. The more forward lean you have, the quicker your board will move from edge to edge.

If you plan on putting down long, arching carves, you want a lot of forward lean. But if you're just learning to ride or you're riding a lot of park, you're better off with less forward lean. Beginner snowboarders should try riding with only a couple degrees of forward lean, or none at all.

To change the amount of forward lean on your bindings, look for the forward lean adjuster on the highback, where it meets the heel cup. Although most of today's bindings allow you to adjust forward lean on the fly, sans screwdriver, certain brands require a Phillips head to do any adjusting.

Once you've learned the basic snowboarding techniques, then mess around with your forward lean. Try out a lot of different angles. There's no way to know what will feel best until you try it, so do some testing. Try out your bindings with tons of forward lean, none at all, and every angle in between. Settle on whatever feels best.

TEN ESSENTIALS

1. Navigation (map and compass)
2. Sun protection (sunglasses and sunscreen)
3. Insulation (extra clothing)
4. Illumination (headlamp or flashlight)
5. First-aid supplies
6. Fire (firestarter and matches/lighter)
7. Repair kit and tools (including knife)
8. Nutrition (extra food)
9. Hydration (extra water)
10. Emergency shelter

The Mountaineers

CHAPTER 2

A snowboarder slashes his way down the mountain at Big Sky, Montana.

Snowboarding 101

Snowboarding is a pretty new pursuit. Sometime around 1965, Sherman Poppen built a Snurfer for his daughter. The Snurfer—its name a portmanteau of "snow" and "surfer"—was essentially a skateboard without wheels. It was steered by a hand-held rope, and large staples were driven into the top of the board for traction. The next year the Snurfer was mass-produced and sold as a toy, and snowboarding was born.

Surfers and skateboarders alike were attracted to the sport. They instantly began pushing the boundaries of the equipment and what could be done with it. Before long, the snowboarding pioneers began rethinking the design of their snowboards. The Snurfer was a good jumping-off point, but it really was more of a toy than the specialized piece of equipment that snowboarders desired. And just like their skate and surf forefathers, snowboarders were quick to embrace the DIY (Do It Yourself) approach.

They wanted better boards, so they built them. During the 1970s and 1980s, Dimitrije Milovich, Jake Burton Carpenter, Tom Sims, and Mike Olson led the snowboard design revolution. Legend says that Milovich, a surfer living on the East Coast, was originally inspired to build snowboards after discovering he could slide sideways on cafeteria trays. He designed boards modeled after the ones he surfed, and he is credited with the idea of adding metal edges to the boards. In 1976 he started Winterstick Snowboards in Utah.

Meanwhile, a young towheaded kid from the Pacific Northwest was building boards in his junior high shop class. Mike Olson realized his calling at a young age and spent the better part of his teenage years developing different board designs and building them in his garage. Olson dropped out of college and went on to start Gnu Snowboards.

At the same time, Jake Burton Carpenter was chasing the ski bum dream in Stratton, Vermont. He paid his bills by pouring drinks at night and poured the rest of his energy into crafting snowboards. "Carpenter" doesn't roll off the tongue like "Burton," so Jake founded Burton Snowboards a few years later.

Tom Sims was also doing more or less the same thing, but over in California. The fuse was lit and burning quickly across the country. Snowboarding was ready to boom.

Every year brought more design innovations. When Jeff Grell developed the highback, bindings changed forever and so did snowboarding. Highbacks allowed snowboarders to control their boards like never before; for the first time, they could lean into their bindings and this greatly improved board control. As a result the level of riding progressed at an unprecedented pace.

However, snowboarders faced a lot of opposition in the early years. Ski resorts didn't know how to react to this new breed, and their first reaction was to ban snowboarding from their slopes, claiming that it was too dangerous and that snowboarders were out of control. Snowboarders were seen as punks and often derided by skiers. In the early 1980s, only 10 percent of ski resorts allowed snowboarders. But snowboarders were passionate about their newfound sport and not about to bow down to the stodgy population of skiers. They kept riding, and in time proved that they deserved the right to ride resorts.

Soon riders were organizing contests and traveling to compete. The first competitions were races, with riders navigating Giant Slalom (GS) gates to see who could get down the course quickest. In 1982 the National Snowboarding Championships were held at Suicide Six Ski Resort in Vermont—marking the start of competitive snowboarding.

A couple of years later, the Mount Baker Resort, across the country in Washington, held the inaugural Banked Slalom. This event still had gates that riders had to ride around, but the course design included banked turns and proved to be more of a true representation of how snowboarders rode.

All the while, snowboarders were learning how to jump, spin, and grab their boards; soon, competitions evolved with more of an emphasis on freestyle. Events started popping up around the United States, then around the world. The first World Cup of Snowboarding was held in 1983, at Soda Springs in California. It marked the beginning of a sea change in competitive snowboarding, as it was the first competition in which riders snowboarded on a man-made half-pipe. Contests began moving away from racing and focusing instead on jumps and on tricks executed in the half-pipe.

These competitions served as a venue for snowboarders to show what they could do. Riders started rising through the ranks, pushing each other further every time they gathered. Freestyle snowboarding proved to be a real crowd-pleaser. The crowds grew bigger. More people took notice of this new sport and decided to try it for themselves. Inevitably, sponsors recognized the potential marketing opportunities and started paying riders to represent their products. Snowboarders were now getting paid to ride; what was once just a hobby was quickly becoming a full-time job.

Craig Kelly is credited for defining what a professional snowboarder could be. He was a fierce competitor, winning almost every event he entered. During his fifteen-year professional career, he won four world championships and three U.S. championships. He also won the Legendary Baker Banked Slalom three times. All this winning and the attention it earned him made his sponsors happy. He boosted his level of exposure even higher by working closely with photographers and getting a lot of editorial coverage. And he did this with all the logos showing, to earn all the incentive checks he could. Kelly figured out how to make a lot of money from snowboarding, and others did their best to keep up.

Then, when he was on top of the game, he walked away from the contest scene. Kelly was always ahead of the curve—and the pack, for that matter. He wanted to ride mountains, not race courses. So that's what he did. The move was unprecedented at the time, but if anyone could step away from the competitive circuit and earn a living by simply riding mountains, Kelly could. He didn't rest on his laurels. Instead, he pioneered big-mountain riding. He rode lines previously considered impossible, in the process creating a niche for pro snowboarders who didn't want to compete to earn a paycheck. Because Kelly was largely regarded as the best snowboarder in the world, everyone wanted to emulate his every move. He took his freestyle skills to the big mountain to push himself and see just what he was capable of. He led, others followed, and the idea of all-mountain freestyle riding was born.

Kelly did things on his snowboard that others could barely comprehend. He went faster, jumped higher, caught more air, and did it all with more style than anyone else.

He pushed the level of riding further than anyone imagined it could go. And he made it look so easy. He rode with grace and his riding laid the groundwork for modern snowboarding as we know it. Kelly died in an avalanche in Revelstoke, British Columbia, in 2003 while training to be a guide for the Selkirk Mountain Guides. His influence can be seen in the style of riders today and he is still regarded as a legend, sometimes referred as the "Godfather of Freeriding."

The late 1980s and early 1990s saw snowboarding really boom. For a few years, literally hundreds of new snowboard companies sprouted up every year. Some observers even argue that this boom saved the American ski industry, at a time when the number of skiers was steadily declining. Resorts now saw an equal if not greater number of snowboarders turning out. Even more sponsors got in on the action, and all the innately talented (if slightly degenerate) teenagers were cashing in.

The new snowboarding superstar was an incredibly nimble Norwegian named Terje Haakonsen. Terje quickly became a hero to snowboarders around the world. He dominated freestyle snowboarding in the 1990s,

Terje Haakonsen set the world record for highest air with this 9.8 meter backside 360 at the 2007 Arctic Challenge in Oslo, Norway. (Photo by Nick Hamilton)

Shaun White on his way to another contest win

winning the ISF World Championships in half-pipe three times, first in 1993, then 1995, and again in 1997. He also won five European championships in half-pipe, and of course there were his three half-pipe wins at the U.S. Open. Tejre, like Craig Kelly, won the Legendary Baker Banked Slalom, but he bested Kelly by winning it six times—in 1995, 1996, 1998, 2000, 2003, and 2004.

Tejre also holds the world record for highest air in a quarter-pipe. He flew 9.8 meters, or about 32 feet, out at the Arctic Challenge in 2007, which is regarded as one of snowboarding's premier events—an event that Tejre helped create. Terje also invented a half-pipe trick called the Haakon Flip. Two films have been made about him: *Subjekt Haakonsen* and *Haakon Factor*.

Today Terje continues pushing snow-boarding and is revered by snowboarders young and old. He's a living legend who

Shaun White took the win at Park City's inaugural Intelligent Design contest, but fellow Burton riders Charles Reid (left, 2nd) and Luke Mitrani (right, 3rd) were hot on his heels.

might not be in the limelight as much any more, but his influence can still be seen in every aspect of snowboarding.

During Terje's heyday the next snowboarding phenomenon was born. Shaun White first strapped into a snowboard at age six. By the time he was seven, he was sponsored by Burton. At twelve he was traveling the world, competing alongside riders twice his age. From the very beginning, it was clear that White would become one of the best snowboarders in the world. It didn't take long to prove it. White, a driven competitor, started winning almost every event he entered and quickly became one of the sport's most decorated riders. The list of his first-place finishes is long, but his most notable achievement is certainly his gold medal at the 2006 Winter Olympics in Torino, Italy.

White's ongoing wins and talent have

elevated him to celebrity status. Rolling Stone magazine declared White "the coolest kid in America." He's appeared in American Express ads alongside Robert De Niro. Target sells a line of clothing designed by his brother and him. He has his own video game. It's not an exaggeration to say that White is his own industry.

And although Shaun White receives some criticism for cashing in on all these non-endemic sponsorship opportunities, the fact remains that he's snowboarding's ambassador to the general public. And we have a good dude representing us. He's down-to-earth, light-hearted, sometimes a wiseass, and never one to take himself too seriously. But he does take snowboarding seriously, and by all indications, he's doing everything he can to continually push his riding further.

Snowboarding is no longer a fringe sport for responsibility-shirking surfers and skaters. Although a vast majority of snowboarders are between the ages of fifteen and twenty-two, the sport is growing and riders of all ages are making their way to the mountains.

For anybody who's dedicated to snowboarding, it's hard to use the word "sport" when talking about snowboarding. Snowboarding is more than that: It's a lifestyle. (It's a cliché, yes, but one that holds true.) There's something about spending time in the mountains, recreating with friends, exploring by board, and constantly pushing your abilities further that makes snowboarding incredibly addicting. To ride is to be free. But be warned: Once you fall in love with snowboarding, other responsibili-ties probably won't seem so pressing.

Snowboarding is decision-making, solitude, adrenaline, disaster, recovery, shared joy, trusting yourself, overcoming fear, testing your abilities, realizing your passion, finding your line, surrendering to the elements, and enlightenment.

Snowboarding offers all of life's most valuable experiences in every run. I'd argue that there's nothing better you can do.

BASIC SNOWBOARDING TECHNIQUES

You've decided to learn to ride. Now the question is where.

You have some options. A resort is undoubtedly the best place to get your feet wet, or rather, snowy. Resorts offer every type of terrain, plus lifts that drop you off at the top of it all. A day at the resort means lunch in the lodge and the option of hot beverages whenever you need them. And you will need them.

The rest of this chapter describes learning basic snowboarding techniques at a resort, which is what most beginning snowboarders do. However, be prepared for your day at the resort to come with a hefty price tag. When you add up gas, lift tickets, food, and sometimes lodgings, a trip to any resort can be a big investment.

One of the biggest complaints about snowboarding at a resort is the cost. It can be prohibitive, discouraging a lot of would-be snowboarders from attempting it. Now more than ever, many riders living in cold enough locations are finding ways to ride

CROSSING OVER FROM SKIING

If you know how to ski, snowboarding will be a lot easier to learn. Skiers understand the fundamentals of how their skis slide on snow, how to stop them, how edges work, what a fall line is, where to go straight, where to turn, and how to stay safe on the mountain. All these skills are key elements of snowboarding. The main difference is the way your body is oriented while sliding, and the fact that your bindings don't release. Contrary to popular belief, in many ways your position on the board and your non-releasing bindings both make snowboarding safer. You're a lot less likely to injure your legs in a snowboarding accident than when skiing, though it's more serious to be strapped to your board in an avalanche.

Snowboarding puts less stress on your knees than skiing. With both of your feet on one board, your weight is evenly distributed between both legs, which translates into less strain on any one leg. What's more, the soft flex of snowboard boots allows for greater range of motion in your ankles, so any impact can be absorbed throughout your entire leg, rather than in just your knee, as is often the case in skiing.

Another advantage of riding a snowboard is that when you fall, you've only got one board to worry about. Unlike in skiing, where your legs are free to go in either direction, in snowboarding your lower body moves as one unit. Since your board can't pop off, you don't have to worry about tracking down errant equipment—not to mention the danger that runaway skis can pose to passersby caught off guard.

But the best thing about snowboarding isn't the dangers you can avoid. It's the thrills you can seek. Skiers typically try to get down the hill as fast and efficiently as possible. Turns are short, and the line is direct. In snowboarding you're encouraged to meander. Carve down the top of the run, slash the banks on the side of the cat track, jump off that little bump over there, ride the fallen tree, do a 180 and practice riding switch. Your objective changes when you ride a snowboard. You are no longer looking for the shortest distance between Point A and Point B. It's not about the path of least resistance but rather the line that looks like the most fun. Snowboarding will make you look at the mountain differently. And if the number of riders out ripping the resorts on boards is any indication, the sideways perspective must be pretty good.

for free. Don't let the cost of resort riding keep you from giving snowboarding a try but also don't go near the backcountry when you're just learning to ride. It's no place for beginners and even intermediate riders should approach it with caution. See Chapter 8 for more about the challenges, rewards, and dangers of backcountry boarding.

Start here.

Time with friends is one of the best things about snowboarding.

TAKING IT TO THE STREETS

Increasingly, riders are simply shredding the streets. Fresh snowfall in the city can offer a resort park riding experience without the price tag. When snow is on the ground, all kinds of man-made features become perfect for snowboarding. Find a hill, maybe one with a rail on it, or a park bench, or picnic table. Build a small jump. And bring your buddies. Just keep in mind that some municipalities may have regulations about what's legal on public property and not every golf course welcomes snowboarders.

Some argue that this isn't real snowboarding, pointing to snowboarders who learn to jump onto rails before they even learn to turn properly. That's a bad attitude. If you're strapped into your snowboard, then you're snowboarding. No one type of riding is better than another. It's all for fun. Never take it too seriously—that will ruin it. The point is to ride, whatever you can, whenever you can, until you can't anymore. It's as simple as that.

You don't need a mountain to snowboard.

SKATING

The first step to learning how to slide on a snowboard is to skate. Skating means strapping in your front foot and using your free back foot to push yourself around. This gives you a feeling for how the board slides on the snow. It will be awkward. The boot on your free foot is sure to feel like a cast. It will feel more normal with time and practice.

Spend some time skating around the base area or the bottom of the beginner slopes on your first day. Push with that

You'll do a lot of skating when learning to snowboard.

back foot, then place it on the board in front of your back binding. This is a great way to feel your board out while still being able to put your foot down if you get off-balance, which you will.

Practicing skating might seem like an unnecessary step, but you will do a lot of it up on the mountain so don't overlook it. As a snowboarder you don't use ski poles; instead you use your back foot to push yourself through the flat sections of the mountain. Skating is as much a part of snowboarding as riding with both feet strapped in.

GETTING ON AND OFF THE LIFT

Getting onto a lift is a big source of anxiety for all snowboarding rookies. Don't worry, as with everything in snowboarding, it only gets easier with time and plenty of practice.

First get comfortable with skating. You'll ride the chairlift with only one foot in your bindings, so if you're comfortable skating, the entire lift-riding experience will be that much easier.

The loading ramps at lifts are notoriously icy and rutted, so approach them with caution, paying extra attention to your board. Sit down on the lift, keeping your board up. Keep the leading edge of your snowboard lifted up slightly until you're off the ground. Then lower the safety bar/footrest and enjoy the ride.

As you approach the top of the lift, line up your board so it's perpendicular to the lift and pointed straight down the off-ramp. Different lifts have different unloading speeds. These days most resorts have high-

Preparing to unload

speed quads, which have room for four riders in each chair. High-speed quads typically slow down quite a bit when unloading. Most fix-grip chairlifts have only two seats per chair and they unload a little faster. Don't worry too much about which type of lift you're riding; simply concentrate on getting on and off smoothly.

The steepness of off-load ramps also varies, and some beginners panic when faced with one of the steeper ones. That's unnecessary: Unloading is a quick process, and you shouldn't overthink it. Put your board on the snow, firmly planting your unstrapped back foot on your board, just in front of your back binding. Keep your knees bent and ride straight away from the lift. Try keeping your hand on the chair.

Push yourself off the lift a little so you get away from the chair and out of the way quickly, to avoid the next chair full of riders. But don't rush the unloading process. Let the chair push you slowly into the down ramp. Stay calm, stand up slowly, concentrate on keeping your board straight, and ride away. It's natural to want to put your back foot down to slow yourself. Resist this urge. You want to slow down on the flat run-out at the bottom of the ramp, so don't attempt to put the brakes on too early because that will probably cause you to fall.

Once you've made it to the bottom of the ramp and are starting to slow your slide, try to stop yourself by turning. Gently and gradually, put pressure on either your heel edge, by raising your toes, or your toe edge, by raising both heels, and turning your upper body in the direction you want to go.

If you do fall while unloading, just get out of the way as quickly as possible. If it's easiest to move off to the side, do that, or go down the ramp if it's quicker that way. It's embarrassing, but it happens all the time. The lift attendants keep an eye out for people falling and they may slow the lift to allow you more time to move out of the way, but don't count on it. Wiggle, shuffle, scoot, or slide out of the way so you don't compound the situation by causing people on the lift behind you to fall, too.

It's hard to practice unloading. If you can find a small slope that flattens out somewhere in the base area, try dropping into the pitch with only one foot strapped in. Start at the top of the small hill in a standing position and then turn your board and body downhill. Put your foot on your board, just in front of your back binding, and slide downhill.

The biggest hurdle to learning to unload from a lift is simply getting used to the sudden rush of speed you get every time you unload. Embrace every opportunity you have to get comfortable riding with only one foot strapped in, and soon you'll be ripping down the lift ramps like a pro.

SIDESLIPPING

After you've skated around a bunch, find a mellow section of the slope, strap both feet in and try sliding on the edge of your board, or *sideslipping*. It will probably feel even more unnatural than skating did, but again it'll get easier with practice.

It's easiest to begin sideslipping on your heel edge, the edge of your board that runs behind your heels. To get a sense of how this feels, stand on a hill without a snowboard strapped to your feet and lift your

Expect to spend a lot of time sideslipping on your heel edge as you're learning to snowboard.

toes. Keep your knees bent and your hands out in front of you for balance. Find the balance point that allows you to keep your toes raised. Now re-create this position while attached to your board. Standing up for the first time will be challenging. You have to balance on your heels and the heel edge of your board. You're bound to fall a lot while learning how to balance on your heel edge. You will have bruises. Don't say you weren't warned—but don't hesitate to get right back up. That's the only way to learn.

The next step is to slide down a slope that you are comfortable with. Start on a moderate slope and then progress to steeper hills as you get better at sideslipping.

To begin sideslipping, sit on the snow with your board downhill in front of you and your hands by your side. Push yourself up with your arms and slowly lean forward. Keep your hands out in front of you for balance. As you're balancing on your heel edge, lower your toe edge to increase the speed of your slide. To reduce your speed, simply raise your toes. This will cause the heel edge of your snowboard to bite into the hill and act as a brake. To allow yourself to slide faster, just lower your toes toward the snow.

It's easy to let one end of your snowboard rotate downhill when you're side-slipping. This is caused by unequal pressure on your feet. When this happens, you end up sliding down the hill at an angle. You don't want this to happen because you're liable to gain too much speed and lose control. To correct this, balance your weight evenly on your legs. Keep

your board edge perpendicular to the fall line and put an even amount of pressure on your feet, so you will be able to slowly sideslip down the run.

The process for sideslipping on your toe edge is much the same, only you balance on your toes and control the speed of your slip with your toe edge. Start out on your knees, facing uphill, and dig your toe edge into the snow. Push yourself up and balance over your toes. Then slowly lower your heels and notice how your speed increases. Raise your heels to apply more pressure to the toe edge and slow down.

Sideslipping can be tough at first, but it gets easier with time and practice. The most important thing is to trust yourself and your ability to balance on either your toe or heel edge.

FALLING LEAF

Once you have figured out sideslipping, the next step is the falling leaf. Essentially, falling leaf is sideslipping from left to right and vice versa, back and forth across the run. You zigzag down the hill. It's a great way to get a feel for your edges.

Start out sideslipping on your heel edge downhill. It's easiest to learn the falling leaf on your heel edge so you can see what's in front of you. Also, if you feel yourself falling, you simply lean back and fall onto your butt.

Shift your weight onto either your front foot or your back foot. Lean into that foot with your upper body, keeping your knees bent and your hands out in front of you for

Use falling leaf to traverse across a run.

balance. If you lean into your front foot, for example, your board will start sliding downhill and in that direction. As you start sliding, turn your head to look in the direction you're headed.

When you want to change direction, shift your weight to the other foot—in this example, your back foot—and turn your head in that direction. You'll start sliding downhill diagonally the other way.

Make sure to stay aware of any uphill traffic, that is, skiers or snowboarders who are uphill of you and headed downhill in your direction. All that zigzagging across the run can put you in harm's way. Don't work on your falling leaf on crowded runs. As you get more comfortable going back and forth in the falling leaf, you can try going faster by angling your board more directly downhill.

Snowboarders at every level, from beginner to expert, use the falling leaf technique. It's a good way to get down steep terrain that might be beyond your ability level because you can take the descent slowly, sliding back and forth down the hill.

TURNING

For many beginning snowboarders, learning to link turns is their first big hurdle. Linking turns means transitioning from a toe-edge turn into a heel-edge turn, then back to a toe-edge turn, and so on and so forth. Turning your board requires you to trust your abilities and commit to lower body movements that feel like they'll send you straight into the snow.

Before you start doing linked turns, you should learn to do skidded turns. A skidded turn is basically a glorified sideslip in which you use your hips and upper body more. The movements are small but they can feel awkward to people new to snowboarding. It's best to practice skidded turns on a run that you're comfortable with.

As you're riding down the run, pick a point downhill where you want to start your turn. To initiate a skidded turn, start by turning your shoulders in the direction you want to go. As your board starts turning, keep pressure on the edge that's in contact with the snow. It doesn't matter if you start out making a toe-edge turn or

Lead with your upper body on heel-edge turns.

heel-edge turn. Let's say you begin making a heel-edge turn. In that case, you keep your weight on your heels by leaning back and lifting up with your toes. For toe-edge turns, lean forward into the slope and put pressure on your toe-edge while lifting your heels. Push your back leg out and downhill, and you'll force your snowboard to skid on one edge.

Once your board is skidding, it'll be just as if you're sideslipping again. A lot of beginners resort to the falling leaf at this point because it can be intimidating to transfer from one edge to another while turning. You should avoid this because the longer you continue doing the falling leaf, the longer it'll take you to learn how to link turns.

When you've completed your skidded turn, ride *flat-based* (not on one edge or the other, but with your board flat against the snow) across the slope with your board pointed slightly downhill. Try another skidded turn when you either want to change direction or are going faster than feels safe. If you're on your toe edge, continue to lift your heels, turning your head, shoulders,

Use your arms for balance when making toeside turns.

and hips in the direction of your turn. Rotating your hips shifts your body weight and helps you push the back end of your snowboard out. While on your toe edge, remember to lean into the run and push your back leg downhill to apply more pressure to your edge and continue your skid. If you're on your heels, the motion is the same but instead you lean back a little and lift your toes. Always keep your knees bent and your hands out in front of you for balance. And, as always, look where you want to go, because your body will follow your head.

Make sure that you allow a few seconds to ride flat-based in one direction before turning in the other direction when linking turns. Turn too quickly and you run the risk of catching the downhill edge of your snowboard on the snow. You will catch your edges while learning to snowboard—everybody does—and you'll fall hard when it happens. As painful as it is, at least it will inspire you to concentrate on keeping your edges up so you can avoid being pitched again.

RIDING SWITCH

Riding switch means riding backward, or treating the foot that's typically your leading foot as your trailing foot. Riding switch is an important skill to have as a snowboarder. When you're learning to ride, there are times when you have to *revert* (turn) to ride regular, but if you can ride switch, you can simply go with the flow. You'll need to know how to ride switch once you head into the park or pipe and start learning tricks, as a lot of the spins put you down in the landings backward.

In short, you need to learn how to ride switch, and the sooner the better. Practice switch riding on a mellow slope. It's best to practice earlier in the day when your legs are fresh.

To start riding switch, simply continue a heel-edge or toe-edge turn 180 degrees, or until what's usually your trailing foot becomes your leading foot.

Once you're in switch riding position, use all the fundamentals you've learned for riding regular and apply them to this new stance. Keep your knees bent, look downhill, and practice turning just like you would otherwise, initiating every turn with your head and shoulders.

The more you ride switch, the more comfortable you'll become shredding both ways. Ultimately this will make you a better snowboarder. Challenge yourself to ride switch for entire runs—or for entire days.

FALLING

Snowboarders fall down. It's just part of the deal. Thankfully, snow is a pretty forgiving surface. If you can, learn to snowboard when there's some new snow because it'll make the impact of falling a little softer and easier on the body. Even a little bit helps. Odds are you won't be afforded the luxury of fresh snow every time you ride, though, so it's important to learn how to fall. It sounds awfully oxymoronic, but learning to fall is crucial in snowboarding. It can save you from injury and allow you to put in more days on snow.

When you're learning to snowboard, the most common cause of falls is catching

Falling is part of snowboarding, so don't forget to laugh at yourself when you are rolling around in the snow.

your edges on the snow. Edges are sharp, and if you don't keep your downhill edge up, then it will hook on the snow and cause you to fall. The trouble with catching your edge—and most falls, for that matter—is that it's almost impossible to anticipate. If you do realize a split second in advance that you're about to take a tumble, try to relax. A relaxed body fares a lot better than a stiff one.

As a rule of thumb, you want to roll with the fall. The beauty of snow is that it's slick, so you can slide out of falls. The more you can keep your momentum going downhill, with the fall, the better off you'll be.

Try to resist the urge to break your fall with your arms. Many snowboarders end up with wrist, arm, and shoulder injuries by putting their arms out when they're going down. It's a hard instinct to fight, but you're better off dispersing the impact to other parts of your body. Instead of reaching out to break your fall, try wrapping your arms around your torso, as if you were giving yourself a hug. That way, your entire upper body takes the impact.

Pads are another great way to lessen the harm you can cause yourself while learning how to snowboard. Lots of snowboard companies make pads that are specifically designed for snowboarders. Butt pads and wrist guards are the most common pads made for snowboarders, as these are the areas that take the most abuse when you're learning. Low-profile knee pads can also be a good idea. Your local snowboard shop should carry them, and the staff can help you figure out which ones are best for you.

Like every aspect of snowboarding, falling only gets better—or, really, less bad—with practice. It's guaranteed that every snowboarder involuntarily practices falling almost every time they ride. So the more you ride, the more you'll fall, and eventually it will get easier to take your lumps.

GETTING UP AFTER YOU FALL

Each time you fall, you need to get up again. The act of pushing yourself back up can make your muscles ache from your thighs to your stomach. You can minimize that pain by knowing how to make getting up a little easier.

You want to get up using your toeside edge. Getting up toeside is easier than heelside because you can lean into the slope and use your hands for support.

After you fall, arrange yourself so that you are on your knees and the toe edge of your board is making contact with the snow. Also, make sure that your board is perpendicular to the slope of the mountain. If your board is slanting down the hill, you'll start sliding away before you're ready.

Now push yourself up like you're doing a push-up. Balance on your toe edge and keep your center of gravity low. Slowly lean back downhill and look over your shoulder at the run below you. You should be able to control your sideslip from this position. Lower your heels to release pressure on your toe edge and start sliding down the run.

You should also learn how to get up on your heelside edge. This method requires more balance. You have to trust yourself because you're leaning downhill and it will feel like you're going to fall forward.

Get up on your heels by moving your butt as close to the board as you can. Your knees will probably be in your chest. Now dig the heel edge of your board into the snow a little bit. Lift your legs and drive them into the snow a few times until you have made a little notch in the snow. The notch can be just a couple inches deep; the idea is to create a semi-flat surface to balance on, which can make a world of difference.

Put your hands on the snow behind you. Push yourself up and then slowly stand up from that squatting position, keeping your center of balance low and right over your heels. Once you're standing, lean forward or push your toes down to release the pressure from your heel edge. Then slide down the hill.

The starting position for getting up on your heelside edge

THE BENEFITS OF SNOWBOARDING LESSONS

A great way to learn how to snowboard and progress in the sport is by taking lessons from an instructor. Most resorts offer lessons through their snowboarding school. You can sign up either for a group lesson (groups usually consist of five to ten people), or you can go for a one-on-one private lesson. If you have the dough, the latter is your best bet.

An instructor can provide you with all the basic, need-to-know information, answer your questions, and explain the techniques. Good instructors also teach you about the gear involved and how to use it properly. I have taught people who started out knowing nothing about snowboarding except that you use one board to do it. In my experience, one lesson can be enough to get you started as a snowboarder.

One major advantage is that an instructor can tell you what you are doing wrong and how to fix it. If you try to learn snowboarding on your own, you might do things wrong without being aware of it. I have instructed people who have gone out a few times on their own before taking lessons, and many of the "techniques" they've learned are incorrect. Even one half-day lesson can give you the right fundamentals to build on. Having an instructor will give you a strong base for developing the most effective techniques and habits.

Another merit of snowboard lessons is learning where to begin. A first-time snowboarder can't just ride the chairlift to the top of the mountain and expect to get down in one piece. Certain steps are necessary to properly progress at snowboarding and work your way toward more advanced techniques. You have to learn small things like how to skate (that is, ride with one foot strapped in) and how to get off the chairlift before taking the big step of going up on the chairlift. An instructor will guide you through each step in the process.

If your first lesson goes well, and you feel comfortable enough to go out on your own the next day, then have a go at it. People progress at different rates. Some people I have instructed learned how to link turns on their first run, and others took a couple hours just to figure how to control their boards. In my five years as a snowboard instructor, I have never had a student who could not link turns by the end of a lesson. By the end of the lesson, I would say more than 95 percent of my students have been stoked on snowboarding and excited to go out the next time.

Private instruction is also a good way for intermediate snowboarders to work on more advanced techniques. If nothing else, an instructor is someone to ride with. I have had clients who were extremely advanced at snowboarding techniques and just wanted someone with them who had a little more knowledge of the mountain. The bottom line is that any instruction helps and can set you on your way to shredding a lot of the mountain in your first few days. What have you got to lose?

Danny Gariepy, certified snowboard instructor,
American Association of Snowboard Instructors

TYPES OF SNOWBOARDING

Now that you have the basic techniques of snowboarding, you're ready to figure out which type of riding suits you best. And the best way to do that is to snowboard as much as you can. Get up to the mountain every chance you get and explore every inch of that snowy playground. Make laps from top to bottom. Cruise through the park. Drop into the pipe and pump the transition. Have fun with it and do what you love. That's what snowboarding is all about.

Floating a backside 180 on the way down the mountain

Today's terrain parks offer something for every level of rider.

ALL-MOUNTAIN RIDING

All-mountain riding is about riding everything at the resort. It's taking laps on groomers (groomed trails), carving turns, popping *ollies*, ducking into the trees, riding the top of the mountain, the bottom and all the runs in between. The skills you need in all-mountain riding apply to every other type of snowboarding you'll do. The best way to become a better snowboarder is to ride it all. Every inch of the resort has a lesson to offer the beginner. Before you go jumping into the park or pipe, concentrate on riding around the resort. Check it all out. Get a feel for how your board performs and how you ride on a variety of terrain. Most importantly, enjoy the freedom of being able to go anywhere you want on the mountain. Once you learn how to get around, it's yours for the shredding. Chapter 3 discusses all-mountain riding in depth.

"Riding the entire mountain is the best way to become a better boarder. The best advice I have for you while you're riding around the mountain is to stay positive and have fun. If you're doing that, things are going to work—it's gonna be good. You'll learn all the skills you need just doing laps all day. Just make sure you keep that 'git 'er-done' mentality and give it your all."

Tim Eddy

PARK RIDING

The specially designed snowboard parks built at resorts are the place to go to work on your tricks. After you feel comfortable riding the rest of the resort, head to the park to push yourself. Park riding requires a good deal of skill and bravery. The features are built for getting air and doing tricks, so beginners better understand that the park is no place to learn to turn. Parks are constantly groomed, so fresh snow is scarce and ultimately there's not as much of the fresh stuff to break your fall. But once you can confidently ride most of the mountain, know how to fall without getting too badly hurt, have an understanding of jumping, and are ready to test your abilities, the park is the place to be.

"You always know what to expect in the park. It's so convenient and it's literally made for you. The park has almost everything you could want to ride. You can start out carving some turns, then move on to some little jumps, and then come the jibs. Riding the park will give you better board control and eventually you'll be able to hit anything that is thrown in front of you."

Desiree Melancon

Riding the pipe with friends makes the learning process all the more fun.

PIPE RIDING

It requires some serious skill to ride the half-pipe. You have to understand transition and be able to use it to your advantage. You also have to be comfortable going fast and transferring from edge to edge quickly. Half-pipes can be intimidating. The snow is typically hard, if not icy. A lot of really strong riders are usually gathered there. And the walls range from 15- to 18- feet high, so it can be hard to imagine getting to the lip, let alone airing out. But half-pipes are also great places to progress. You can start small, get comfortable, and work your way up, going faster and jumping higher with every run. And then, of course, you hike up and do it all again.

"Pipe riding is tough, which is why it's a great way to push yourself. You can't just cruise through the pipe. You have to really be on it and you have to want it. Sessioning the pipe will make you a better rider, period. When you're learning, remember not to edge too hard. Just let the pipe take you. It can be scary, but with time you'll figure it out. Just remember to always keep your eyes on the prize."

Jed Anderson

BACKCOUNTRY RIDING

Riding in the backcountry could be considered the holy grail of snowboarding. To the beginner it might seem unattainable, but with enough knowledge, the right skills, and a willingness to expend a lot of energy to get to the goods, you too can see what lies beyond the boundaries of the resort. Snowboarders flock to the backcountry for a lot of reasons. They go to escape the crowds, to find new terrain, and to ride in peace and quiet. But most often they go looking for fresh snow. Before you even consider heading out of bounds, you need to be proficient at riding powder and you need to know a great deal about avalanches, weather, and all the other dangers associated with the backcountry. To become a backcountry snowboarder, you must first realize you'll need to approach the backcountry with a lot of respect and understand how much you have to learn.

"I think that one of the most important lessons that I have learned along the way is that when dealing with the backcountry, no matter what someone says, no matter what the snow does when it is ridden, no matter how prepared you think you are, the mountain has the final say. I love to snowboard in the backcountry because it allows me to take my snowboarding to another level, which is where I want to take it. The backcountry is where snowboarders go to push the limits of what we thought was possible."

Patrick McCarthy

Solitude and a heelside slash in the Montana backcountry

CHAPTER 3

The mountain is what you make of it. Have fun.

All-Mountain Riding

In snowboarding, like many things in life, it's better to be well-rounded. Learning to ride all over the entire resort, rather than just one specific discipline like park or pipe, is the best way to progress. What's more, the skills you learn riding around the resort will transfer to the park and pipe, making your transition into these areas that much easier.

You can come across an almost infinite number of obstacles, features, conditions, and situations while riding around the mountain, and each one will help make you a better rider. Terrain parks and half-pipes are fairly controlled environments. They are meticulously maintained: The snow is groomed and all the features are clearly marked. In the park and pipe, what you see is what you get. But out on the rest of the mountain, a lot of trails go ungroomed, obstacles and features aren't always marked, and the conditions are constantly changing.

Imagine what you can learn in one run. Just cruising the groomed trails lets you work on your edge control, turning, switch riding, and going faster. Ducking into the trees teaches you to think two turns ahead and helps you hone your reaction time, not to mention enlightening you about all the snow conditions you can encounter in the woods.

When it comes to all-mountain riding, remember that old adage: What doesn't kill you makes you stronger. Riding the entire mountain will make you a stronger rider. So if you want to improve every aspect of your snowboarding, ride it all, top to bottom, first chair to last.

UNDERSTANDING THE MOUNTAIN ENVIRONMENT

Mountains are wild. Anytime you're in the mountains you are out of your element, and you should approach any day of snowboarding with a healthy dose of humility. You never know what you're going to encounter while riding, so you've got to be ready for anything.

Being in unfamiliar surroundings shouldn't scare you but rather inspire you to become more observant. Never let your guard down while riding. Take it all in, almost to the point of hyper-awareness. If you start feeling overwhelmed by the winter environment, stop and take a seat out of harm's way. Collect your thoughts and remind yourself to just take it one turn at a time. There are many variables out on the mountain, but if you know what things to look out for, no situation should catch you completely off guard.

WEATHER

Weather can play a huge role in your safety. You need to make decisions based on the weather the minute you set foot on the mountain, if not before. Being out in the elements requires that you dress properly and protect yourself from the cold. But just because you're bundled up and feeling relatively warm doesn't mean you can let your guard down. On mountains, the weather can change in a matter of minutes, so always be ready for the worst. That might mean carrying an extra layer of clothing, a hat, gloves, hand-warmers, or snacks. It also means thinking about what you'll do if you get caught out in the cold in nasty weather.

The weather determines more than just what you wear. Stormy weather can limit visibility and turn an otherwise easy run into one that you can't get down. Whiteouts happen, and vertigo is a very real sensation when snowboarding. If you end up in a blizzard, barely able to see your mitten in front of you, proceed with caution, staying close to the people you're riding with.

Always pay close attention to the subtle variances in the snow. A run can look

Remember to stop and look around. Always be aware of your surroundings.

perfectly groomed, but if the light—or the lack of it—is playing tricks on your eyes, you might be headed into terrain that's not as well maintained as it appears. Having the right goggles for the conditions helps you see everything in front of you. Use darker lenses when it's sunny and clear or yellow-tinted lenses when it's storming and visibility is low.

While being aware of your immediate surroundings, always remember to scan the run ahead for any possible dangers. Treat every run like a game of chess, constantly thinking a couple of turns ahead while still remaining focused on the move at hand.

SNOW CONDITIONS

When you're riding the entire mountain, snow conditions vary a lot more than when you're lapping the park and pipe. On a good day at the right resort, you can shred just about every type of snow. (Well, that might be exaggerating—there's an almost infinite number of forms that snow can take—but you get the idea.) When you get off the lift and start sliding on some freshly groomed hard pack, you're forced to pay attention to your edges and work on your balance. Then you might drop into the run and discover it's a chunky face of chopped-up snow. To successfully navigate the ruts and bumps and otherwise

Dark clouds on the horizon mean one thing: Bad weather is rolling in.

less-than-ideal conditions, you have to constantly scan the run in front of you, reacting quickly to each new obstacle. Then, when you turn off into the trees, you may discover untouched powder. Now you have to change your riding posture entirely and pay even closer attention to your surroundings.

And you're only halfway down the run.

Snow conditions vary from the top of the mountain to the bottom, from one run to the next, from the beginning of the day to the end, and from the first day of the season to the last. You never know exactly what to expect when you go snowboarding, but the more often you go, the easier it becomes

to anticipate what kind of snow you will be riding.

The more observations you make about the snow, the better you'll be at riding it. Notice how the temperature, wind, sun, and other natural forces affect the snow. If it's sunny and warm, you can expect the snow to be slushy and you'll move slower. Or, if it's really cold, that snow could turn into a sheet of ice. Just as no two snowflakes are alike, no two days of snowboarding are alike. The most important thing to do is notice how it feels to ride the different types of snow. Figure out what kind of snow you enjoy riding the most, and then seek and destroy.

ALL-MOUNTAIN TECHNIQUES

All-mountain riding means being faced with all kinds of challenges. You have to ride different types of snow and navigate through a variety of types of terrain. Each time you start again at the top of the mountain, you can pick a slightly different line to follow down to the bottom. Part of all-mountain riding is learning how to flow a line, riding

HOW TO CHOOSE A LINE

Personally, I look for lines that I can play around on. I like to have fun and really play when I snowboard, but at the same time, I like to be safe. When scouting a line, I first look at the flow of the line and decide if I can flow it. Then I look for the hazards. In my head I'll go through what things can go wrong and what I would do if each one happened. I really study the run-out because you can hardly ever see that from the top of the line. Then I study the markers that will help me with the line, like trees, rocks, and other snow features. These things help me line up in the right spot when I am at the top about to drop in.

Know your exit before you enter.

When I get to the top, I make sure I still feel good about the line. Sometimes I feel good about it at the bottom, but when I get to the top, I don't feel so good. I've bailed plenty of times on doing a line because I felt it looked sketchy when seen from the top. At the bottom I thought it would be good and safe, but when I got to the top, it wasn't.

This is important. If you don't feel good doing a line when you are standing on the top, then don't do it.

I usually throw snowballs down the face to check the snow. These snowballs give me some idea about the trajectory I need to hit the landing. I also line myself up by talking to a friend at the bottom. Having someone you trust on the other end to help you figure out if you're in the right spot is really important. It can boost your confidence, too.

Remember that not everyone sees the same thing. You should pick a line that you know you can do, not a line that someone else can do. Listen to others who give you good advice about being safe on the line. Don't listen to people who are only telling you to get rad. And always ride within your ability.

Dave Downing, professional snowboarder

If you find yourself in the air, enjoy it.

it smoothly without hesitation, all the way from top to bottom.

To ride the whole resort, you have to be confident riding both switch and regular, popping ollies, sneaking through tight trees, letting it rip in wide-open powder fields, and even dropping cliffs. The beauty of riding the entire mountain is that no two runs are the same, and by snowboarding on new terrain every run you learn something new every time you drop in.

POWDER RIDING

Riding powder can be bliss. It can also be a pain in the ass. Powder could very well be the most frustrating thing for beginner snowboarders. You can see everyone else enjoying all that fresh snow, but you can't figure out how to surf like they do. Be warned: You can expect to wallow in a lot of snow when you're first learning how to ride pow. Don't let those first powder experiences discourage you. Once you learn to float on all that fresh snow, you will know what snowboarding is all about.

Most of the time snow is a fairly firm, almost hard surface, but powder snow is incredibly soft and almost fluid, semi-suspended in the air. Fresh snow creates resistance, so it slows you down. Keep this in

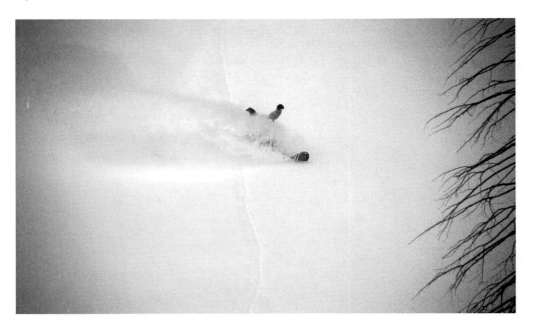

Hacking into a foot of fresh snow

mind whenever you're coming up to flatter sections of the mountain. If the slope is mellowing out and there's a lot of new snow, you need to go fast and point your board straight downhill. That way you don't get stopped by, and then stuck in, the powder.

Your board is designed to float in fresh snow, so let it. Point it downhill and let gravity take control. With practice, you can stop very easily and quickly in powder, so don't be afraid to go fast when there's fresh snow.

More than anywhere else on the mountain, or in any other snow conditions, you need to use your entire body to turn your board while riding powder. On groomed trails you mainly use your lower body to turn, but in powder you really have to lean into every turn and use your upper body to drive through the snow. Instead of slipping from side to side, you want to flow down the hill, linking one turn to the next. Once you get the hang of it, you may find it easier than turning on hard pack because you don't have to rely on your edges as much.

If the fresh snow is really deep, you might want to set the stance on your board back (i.e., move your bindings closer to the tail). A setback stance gives you more nose on your board, allowing your board to float on the snow and turn more easily.

Stay low to navigate around the trees.

Another way to keep the nose of your board up and floating on the snow is to change your riding posture a little. Try leaning back and putting more weight on your back foot.

Riding powder can be exhausting, so don't feel guilty for taking more lodge breaks than usual on a pow day. After all, riding pow is more about the quality of runs than the quantity.

RIDING IN THE TREES

The trees are a great place to ride. It's quiet. The snow is usually deeper and less tracked. And navigating through the woods tests all your skills as a snowboarder. But shredding in the trees carries its own set of risks. You have to commit to riding aggressively when you decide to duck into the trees. You might be able to get away with cruising lackadaisically down the groomers, but once you're in the trees you need to be on point and concentrate on your every move. There are many obstacles to get hung up on, literally, so you need to be able to react quickly. Tree limbs are notorious for jumping out at you. Don't even think about taking your goggles off; you need all the protection you can get when bobbing and weaving through a thick forest.

To learn how to ride in the trees, start on gladed runs. A gladed run is one that has been selectively thinned by the resort to allow you more room to maneuver. If your resort does not have a gladed run, then scout the mountain for some trees that are well spaced. Pick an area that you feel confident about getting through the trees without too much trouble. Make as many laps as you can in the trees, pushing yourself by going faster with every run.

When you feel ready, find some steeper and tighter trees. When riding in the trees, stay especially low and keep a compact riding posture. Sometimes it helps to keep your hands in front of your upper body and face to swat away tree limbs. Always travel downhill a little slower when you're in the trees.

It's also important to look a couple of turns ahead. Concentrate on the snow and look for lines, instead of focusing on the trees. Your body will follow your head, so make sure you're looking at the space between the trees, rather than at the trees themselves.

One more tip: Bring friends. It's never a good idea to ride alone, especially anywhere you might not be found. When riding with friends, always space yourselves out evenly. Give each other enough room to manueuver safely through the trees. Keep an eye out for each other and continually whistle, shout, or otherwise communicate with each other. Make sure everyone is keeping up, and wait for anyone who falls behind. Besides being safer, riding with buddies is also more fun. You're there to help each other when things go wrong or to celebrate when everything is going right.

Don't forget to stop and stand in awe from time to time, too. Being surrounded by giant snow-covered trees is a great reminder of how small we are in the grand scheme of things. That's an important lesson that snowboarding teaches us.

A snowboarder uses the side of the run to blast an air and crank a method.

JUMPING

Catching air is one of the most exciting things you can do on a snowboard. The sensation of popping off the snow, flying for a minute (or more like a second), finding your way back down to the snow, landing cleanly, and riding away is something else. Enlightening, maybe. And learning how to jump really isn't that hard. Particularly proficient first-timers can jump on their first day.

The most basic jump and the start of every snowboard trick is the *ollie*, which is essentially like doing a squat and jumping up into the air, only you lift your leading leg first.

To learn to ollie start on a mellow slope where you can slide slowly downhill. Squat down with your legs bent and leap up, pulling your leading (front) leg up first, then your back leg. When you flex your board in this jumping motion, you store energy in its wooden core. By pulling your back leg up when jumping, you release the energy stored in the flex of your board. For example, if you took a long tree limb and flexed it in the middle, when you released the middle of the limb it would snap back at you. A snowboard works the same way.

Looking for a good transition

Once loaded with flex, it will pop back when the pressure is released. You flex the board by pulling up on your front leg, then jump up with your back leg and suck your knees up as high as possible to make the board pop off the ground.

One of the most important things with ollies is to keep all your movements fluid. You want all the little steps to blend into one. Think of each part as being connected to the others, and all of them working together to create one quick movement.

Once you've mastered the ollie on rela-tively flat slopes, try moving uphill to some-where with more pitch and possibly little mounds of snow to jump, or *pop*, off. Every mountain is littered with things to jump off. Once you learn to jump, you start seeing jumps everywhere. Groomed runs with big rollers (large piles of snow that are groomed in a smooth arc) are good. So are the sides of snowcat tracks. Tree stumps covered in snow also make perfect little platforms to launch off.

But before you go throwing yourself off everything you can get your board on, make sure you scout the landing. Too often, over-zealous snowboarders fly off jumps with no idea what's on the other side. The best jumps have smooth takeoffs and steep landings. You always want to make sure anything you're going to jump off has a landing, or *transition*.

Transition is any change in the angle or pitch of the snow. Transition is your friend. It's where you want to take off from and where you want to land. Essentially, transitions are designed to match your path of flight so as to provide a smooth landing.

Think of Evel Knievel jumping hundreds of feet on a motorcycle. Because the landing ramps he built matched the angle of his flight path, he was able to touch down smoothly and ride away. It's like when you toss a water balloon: The person trying to catch it must move to match its flight path in order to catch it without it popping.

Transition is the slope that catches you on your snowboard. If you jump in the air on your snowboard from flat ground, the impact as you land back on the flat surface will be severe. But if you jump and land on a downhill section of the slope, you can match your board to the angle of the hill and lessen the impact of your landing. The more you ride, the better understanding of transition you will have. Land flat enough times and you'll realize why transition is so important.

Learning to jump might be awkward at first, but with practice it'll feel more natural. Once you've got the fundamentals of jumping figured, work on your style in the air. As you leave the lip of the jump, bring your knees up to your chest, drop your arms by your side and try to stay as compact as possible for as long as you can. Grab your board and keep your body movements to a minimum. Remember, fluid movements off the jump make for fluid ollies and subsequently more control in the air.

GRABS

Grabbing, predictably enough, is when you reach down and grab the board. It's not essential in snowboarding. The bindings do a fine job of keeping the board attached to your feet. Instead, grabbing your board helps you stay compact in the air. It lets you spin more quickly and keeps you from flailing in flight.

You can grab with either your *leading hand* or your trailing hand. Your leading hand is the one that's downhill when you're riding, and your *trailing hand* is the one that's uphill.

You want to grab your board after you've left the lip of the jump and brought your knees up. Hold your grabs for as long as possible, but don't hold them so long that they keep you from extending your legs for the landing.

When it comes to grabbing, anything goes, really. There are a lot of different grabs out there, and you can spend a lifetime trying to learn and perfect them all. Begin by focusing on the ones that feel most natural to you.

Tail Grab. Grab the tail of your board with your trailing hand.

Nose Grab. Grab the nose of your snowboard with your leading hand.

Grabbing melon and spinning a backside 180

A tail grab at a lonely resort in Lebanon

Japan Air. Grab the toe edge of your board just inside your front foot with your leading hand and pull the board back behind you.

Indy. Grab your board between your bindings on the toe edge with your trailing hand.

Indy Nosebone. Straighten your front leg while doing an Indy grab.

Mute. Grab your toe edge between your bindings with your leading hand.

Mute Nosebone. Straighten your front leg while doing a mute.

Stalefish. Grab your heel edge between your bindings with your trailing hand.

Melon. Grab your heel edge between your bindings with your leading hand.

Method. As when doing a melon, you grab your heel edge between your bindings with your leading hand, but then you kick your legs out and/or forward.

DROPPING CLIFFS

Mountains are giant piles of rocks and—depending on the winter and how much snow has fallen—not all those rocks get completely covered up. This is a good thing. The exposed rocks on the mountain are really fun to jump off as long as there's some transition to land on.

Although the word "cliff" might evoke images of 100-foot sheer walls, a cliff is really any vertical drop created by a cluster of rocks. Cliffs can be two feet tall or twenty. It's best to start on the two-footers and then work your way up from there. Once you learn the fundamentals of dropping a small cliff, you can take what you know and gradually apply it to bigger and bigger drops.

As with any jump, always scout your landing before you go flying off a cliff. Ride around the bottom of the cliff first and really look at the landing. Ask yourself some questions: Is the landing steep enough to allow for a relatively smooth touchdown? Is there enough room on the run-out to allow you to stop? Are there any rocks or other obstacles in the landing? Is the snow soft enough that you won't get hurt if you fall in the landing?

The cliff doesn't have to be huge for you to consider all these things. To learn how to drop cliffs, start on some smaller drops and get a feel for falling. You want to land more

Jump off cliffs only if they have steep landings.

on your back foot and the tail of your board, rather than square on both feet. Landing more on your tail helps you keep the nose of your board up. If the nose sinks too far under the snow, you're liable to get pitched forward and sent into a cartwheel.

You're better off doing a small ollie off the top of the cliff, which will allow you to suck your knees up and get into the compact body position you want any time you're catching air. Grabbing your board will help you stay compact in the air; use any grab that feels natural and that you're really comfortable with.

The first time you drop a cliff will be a little unnerving. You'll probably fall through the air for a longer time than you expected, so do your best to keep your body compact and quiet. When dropping cliffs, it's particularly important to not flail around in the air. Again, fluid movements make for fluid airtime.

BUILDING A JUMP

First, find a steep landing, preferably a slope that's 30 degrees or steeper in angle. Work from there to figure out the best spot to build your jump. Sometimes it makes more sense to build the jump closer to the landing, making it more *poppy* (that is, it has a steeper trajectory and will send you higher in the air). If the landing is not too steep, you want to make the takeoff flatter, so you should build the jump farther back. Whatever you do, you and your friends should first agree on a plan.

Then make sure it's a safe spot for a jump. Check that there isn't any exposure above it. Make sure the landing is safe, with no rocks under the snow; landing on rocks is probably the worst thing that can happen to you on a jump.

Build the jump with blocks of snow. The best snow conditions for jump-building are a good, solid snowpack under the powder, so you can build with solid chunks of snow. It's hard to build jumps when it's all sugar or powder snow. Snow with more moisture in it is always better for jumps. It helps to have a big metal shovel and, if the layers of snow are pretty solid, a saw as well. Use those tools to carve out the chunks of snow. Finally, it's also good to have music and (most importantly) some motivated friends to help you.

Make good, solid blocks of snow and stack them like bricks. It's really like building an igloo. Stack the blocks to the height that you want and then fill in the middle with snow. Be sure to build a solid wall around the jump. Snowshoes are super for packing snow on the takeoff and in the run-in. Finally, smooth out the takeoff with your board.

Jussi Oksanen, professional snowboarder

CHAPTER 4

Sunny days make for slushy snow and great park riding.

Park Riding

Not long ago, snowboarders had to fight to have terrain parks at resorts. Since snowboarding has its roots in a trick-centric pursuit like skateboarding, it's only natural that snowboarders would look at the mountain as more than something to carve down. Thanks to the explosion of snowboarding over the last decade, resorts around the world have recognized the value of building parks and catering to shreds' shared desire to jump, spin, and flip their way down the hill. Today, resorts have entire departments dedicated to the building and maintaining of terrain parks. A lot of thought goes into building a jump, placing a rail, or pushing up any number of other snow features.

For the beginner or intermediate rider, the specially designed parks found at resorts offer a perfect jumping-off point. It should go without saying that riding in these parks is serious business. A terrain park is not the place to learn how to link turns. Before you even think about dropping into the park, you should feel confident in your ability to ride fast, stop quickly, turn on a dime, jump, and land. Although some parks might seem geared toward the beginner crowd, any terrain park requires at least an intermediate skill set. Simply put: Unless you've graduated from the bunny slopes, you have no business riding the terrain park.

Like with every new pursuit, park riding is best learned in baby steps. Start small, work your way up, hone your skills elsewhere on the mountain, and then, when you're feeling completely competent, make your way toward the terrain park. It could take you a season to get to that point, or maybe you're a quick learner and will feel ready in a couple of months. You'll know when you're ready, and when that day comes, be prepared to take some thumps. As anyone who has ridden a park will tell you, the park is a great place to bruise your ego ... and the rest of your body.

Cruising through the park at Breckenridge, Colorado

SMART STYLE

The National Ski Areas Association (NSAA) and Burton Snowboards started a terrain park safety initiative recently called "Smart Style." NSAA and Burton worked with the Professional Ski Instructors of America (PSIA) and the American Association of Snowboard Instructors (AASI) to create the Smart Style initiative in hopes of making terrain parks a safer place to ride and keeping riders on their feet and out of the emergency room.

Four main messages are associated with Smart Style:

1. **Make a Plan.** As with most undertakings in life, riding a terrain park always goes more smoothly when you have some idea what you want to do. Any time you head into the park, decide what it is you want to accomplish that day. Set goals for yourself and your riding, and work up to those goals slowly.

2. **Look Before You Leap.** It's never good to go into any situation blindly, especially activities like snowboarding that are inherently risky. Any time you drop into a terrain park for the first time, take at least a run or two to see what's in store. Check out all the jumps, jibs, rails, and any other features you plan on trying. See what the takeoff and landing look like. Try to get an idea about how much speed you'll need to clear said features.

3. **Easy Style It.** Start small and work your way up. You might feel confident in your abilities, but that doesn't mean your body is really ready to huck. Take some warm-up laps. Get your legs back underneath you. Start with some tricks you're comfortable with and then, as the snow softens and your muscles stretch, start to push yourself.

4. **Respect Gets Respect.** Give it and you'll get it. Terrain parks tend to get crowded and—as in any congested place—people's patience gets tested. The golden rule applies to snowboarding, too. Don't cut off other people, and they'll reciprocate the respectful behavior. We're all in this for the same reason, fun, so there's no reason to ruin your day or anyone else's on the hill.

UNDERSTANDING WEATHER

Although an immaculately groomed and maintained terrain park might seem like the last place you'd have to worry about the weather, in fact the weather can strongly affect the way you ride. Everything from changes in temperature, to dustings of snow, to wind can drastically change the way the features ride. A run that's icy and fast in the morning can turn to slush and be slower than molasses come afternoon.

A couple of inches of fresh snow can change the speed for every feature you roll up to. And gusting winds can literally blow you off course, especially when you're in the air.

None of these factors should be taken lightly. If you figure out the speed for a jump and then the conditions change, you could overshoot the deck and land flat, or maybe come up too short and land on the *knuckle* (the last foot or so of the deck, which is too flat to land on). Either scenario could mean an early ending to your day.

Approach every run through the park as if it were your first. Tune into the conditions. If it's cold in the morning and warm in the afternoon, know that the consistency of the snow is changing too, and adjust your riding accordingly. If it's dumping snow, maybe you should work on your all-mountain riding skills instead. Or, if a howling wind is ripping up the run, keep an eye on the flags the park crew has installed on the jumps; those flags can key you in on which way the wind's blowing. Just because the park seems like a controlled environment doesn't mean it is; you should never let your guard down.

PARK FEATURES

Terrain parks are filled with transitions, or in the parlance of snowboarders, *tranny*. Snowboarders are now going bigger than ever in terrain parks, and this escalation can be attributed to advancements in the equipment used to build parks. These advancements have allowed park designers to build bigger transitions.

A good rule of thumb is the more transition the better. Longer transitions offer more room for error. If you go too big or too small on a jump and it has a short transition, you're liable to end up landing on a section of slope that is too flat for your trajectory. Flat landings equal painful impact.

Those new to park riding sometimes don't understand transition and as a result send themselves off jumps that are too small for the speed they're going. If you're going the right speed you should be able to come down in the transition of a landing and feel little to no impact. As you're learning how to handle your speed on jumps, watch other riders who are similar in stature to you. Pay attention to exactly where they drop in, how many turns or speed checks they make, and how hard they pop off the lip.

Park builders know what they're doing. They strive to build jumps that allow for ample amounts of airtime and can accommodate the inevitable fall. Like any playground, terrain parks offer a wide variety of features that serve an equally wide variety of purposes.

TABLETOPS

The most common feature in a park is the traditional *tabletop*. This is a jump that has a lip, a section of flat area (or deck), and a landing. Tables take on all different shapes and sizes, but essentially the idea's the same: At the right speed, your jump will send you on a trajectory that should allow you to touch down smoothly and with minimal impact on the landing.

HIPS

Like tabletops, these features are built for air. The difference is that on a hip the landing is perpendicular to the lip. Hips are great places to learn how to jump because they allow you to start small and go bigger and bigger on every lap, without adding a lot more speed. Hips are also usually built with a lot more transition, which is always a good thing when you're learning to jump.

When you're ready to catch some air try taking it to the hips in the park.

RAILS

Terrain park rails come in an infinite number of varieties. These days, most park crews fabricate their own rails, and this has turned the design of these steel structures into a veritable art form. The basic types (in order of difficulty) are:

Flat rails. Rails that are set up flat, or with little to no downhill pitch.

Down rails. Rails that are set up at a downhill angle, like handrails on a set of stairs.

Flat-down rails. Rails that start out flat and then angle downhill.

Down-flat-down rails. Rails that are angled downhill at first, then kink and flatten out and then angle downhill again, like a handrail on a double set of stairs.

C- or S-shaped rails. These rails curve in one direction or the other, making the shape of the letter C or S.

Rails are either round or flat bars. Round rails are like those used as handrails. They're cylindrical and typically a couple inches in diameter. Flat rails are just that—flat—the sliding surface is usually a couple inches wide. In general, flat rails are easier than round rails because your board can sit flush on them, which makes it easier to balance. Any decent park should have rails for all ability levels. Sliding a rail is a truly unique sensation. It requires a lot of practice and a good deal of bravado, but once you get the hang of it, it'll probably be easier than you imagined.

FUN BOXES

These aptly named box-like sliding surfaces are the best place to learn to slide on something other than snow. Fun boxes are typically eight inches to a foot in width and constructed of both steel and plastic. They're easy to balance on and usually set up in ways that shreds of any skill level can enjoy.

For the beginner who is learning to slide rails, wide fun boxes are a great place to start.

WALL RIDES

Wall rides are another common feature of terrain parks. They're simply walls of varying heights and widths that are built for riding. Wall rides are pretty user-friendly because they're usually built on top of transition, so you can start slow and carry more and more speed into them every time.

Wall rides like this one are designed to be slid or stalled on with your snowboard.

JIBS

A jib is any and everything that can be tapped, slapped, bonked, or slid on a snowboard. A picnic table can be a jib, as can a tree, or an overturned garbage can. Pretty much anything can be a jib. Essentially anything in the terrain park that could be characterized as miscellaneous junk is a jib.

Jibbing a log at Breckenridge, Colorado

ZONES

While the features described above vary a great deal, they all have four basic zones.

Approach zone

This is also called the *in-run*. It can range from a couple of feet to a couple hundred yards, depending on the size of the feature. Regardless of the length of the approach, this is the place where you set up for the feature, bending your knees, centering your balance, clearing your mind, and preparing for takeoff.

Takeoff zone

Also called the *lip* or *jump*, this is the part of the feature designed to launch you into the air or onto the fun box, rail, wall ride, or jib. This is an area of transition. The takeoff will be proportional to the size of the feature, so the bigger the jump, the bigger the takeoff.

Maneuver zone

This is the area where you're away from the snow, either sliding a box or rail, or flying through the air on a table or hip. When you find yourself in the maneuver zone, stay confident in your ability and keep your body compact and quiet. Odds are if you've

This jump at Park City, Utah shows all the zones you'll find on any man-made park feature.

made it this far and you're still upright and traveling in the right direction, you're doing something right, so just keep doing what you're doing.

Landing zone

This is another area of transition. Like the takeoff zone, the landing zone should match the size of the feature. Landings are designed to make it easy for you to touch down and ride away cleanly. You should be able to land with the base of your board flat on the snow and not feel too much impact.

Or, if you end up off-balance, a nice long landing at least helps break your fall.

JUMPING IN THE PARK

The snowboard park is a great place to learn how to jump. Every well-built park should have a wide variety of jumps for snowboarders of all ability levels. But just because there are massive jumps at your disposal doesn't mean you should go flying off them first thing. It's important to start

---

TERRAIN PARK RESPONSIBILITY CODE

Most terrain parks post signs bearing the following safety message, which is endorsed by the National Ski Areas Association:

"Freestyle terrain may contain jumps, hits, ramps, banks, fun boxes, jibs, rails, half-pipes, quarter-pipes, snowcross, bump terrain and other constructed or natural terrain features. These features are provided for your enjoyment and offer adventure, challenge, and fun. However, freestyle terrain use, like all skiing and riding, exposes you to the risk of serious injury. Prior to using freestyle terrain, it is your responsibility to familiarize yourself with all instructions and warnings, and to follow the 'your responsibility' code.

1. Freestyle terrain contains man-made and natural terrain variations.
2. Freestyle terrain changes constantly due to weather and use.
3. Inspect freestyle terrain before using and throughout the day.
4. In jumping and using this terrain, you assume the risk of serious injury.
5. Be courteous and respect others.
6. One user on a terrain feature at a time.
7. Never jump blindly—use a spotter when necessary. Look before you leap!
8. It is your responsibility to control your body on the ground and in the air.
9. Always clear the landing area quickly.
10. Always ride or ski in control and within your ability.

Know the code. It's your responsibility."

Cracking an ollie at Bear Mountain, California

small and work your way up. Try each one of these tricks on a mellow run first. Learn what it feels like to spin around on snow. Then practice them on the small jumps. Get comfortable leaving the lip, flying through the air, grabbing, and landing. Only then should you take it to the medium-size jumps. Repeat the process and progress at a safe pace.

STRAIGHT AIRS

A *straight air* is when you go off the jump and land in the same direction you were going when you left the lip. You don't rotate at all, but just fly through the air straight from the lip to the landing. Straight airs are the first trick any beginner should learn. Knowing how to jump straight gives you the foundation on which to build all the rest of the tricks.

With any straight air, you want to ride into the jump centered over your board, more or less flat-based. If you have too much weight on your toe edge, you could end up leaning over in the air; if you've got all your weight on your heels, you'll probably end up sitting back or leaning back in the air, and letting your legs get above your body. This will typically cause you to land on your butt or back.

As you leave the lip, pop an ollie. Suck your knees up and drop your upper body down to your board. The motion should be nice and smooth. Keep your knees up and your arms down, and try not to flail around a lot.

Once you're in the air, the grab is up to you. Do whatever grab feels natural. You don't have to grab at all. Just doing clean ollies off the jump is a good way to get a feel for being in the air and staying composed. On the other hand, grabbing your board helps keep your body compact and can help you stay composed. So grab it, but don't force it.

As you're coming into the landing, let go of your grab and start to extend your legs. Keep your knees sucked up as long as possible so you can make any needed adjustments while coming into the landing. Then, just before you land, extend your legs so you can absorb the impact with your knees. Strive to put your board down flat-based. Match your board to the angle of the transition on your landing. Stay low, absorbing the landing with your knees and core, and ride straight away.

Halfway through a frontside 180 at Great Divide, Montana

"Once you take off, you don't want to force it. Straight airs are all about just letting the board float up into your hand and staying composed in the air."

Pat Moore

FRONTSIDE 180s

After you've learned how to do a straight air, the frontside 180 is the next trick to check off your list. A 180 is half of a rotation. You spin your body 180 degrees and land riding in the opposite direction from how you left the lip. If you're a regular-footer, you leave the lip with your left foot forward, rotate 180 degrees and land with your right foot forward; it's vice versa for a goofy-footer.

To get a feeling for the motion of a 180, try doing one on the snow without leaving the ground. Frontside 180s are easy, and the first step is convincing yourself of this. Confidence is key when it comes to park riding.

As you approach the jump, stay low and transfer your weight onto your heels. You want to leave the lip of the jump at a slight angle, but because the rotation is so minimal for a frontside 180 you don't need to make much of a set-up turn. Just ride into the jump as you would for a straight air but with slightly more pressure on your heels.

Then, as you leave the lip, initiate the spin with your shoulders. Again, this trick requires very little movement, so don't overdo it by throwing your shoulders into too aggressive a spin. Basically, you just want to leave the lip, turn your shoulders so they're perpendicular to fall line of the landing, and let your legs follow.

The best thing about frontside 180s is that you're able to see the landing ahead of you the entire time. Keep your knees sucked up and your upper body bent over slightly. Front 180s look great with no grab, but if you want to grab, a nose, frontside, mute, or stalefish grab should come naturally.

As you get closer to the landing, finish the full 180-degree rotation so that you can land flat-based and with equal weight on both legs. As you land, turn your head and look downhill. You might feel the urge to look back uphill, but looking down the landing and ahead of you will help you ride away cleanly.

> "I like to really exaggerate the motion of bringing my knees up to my chest when I do frontside 180s. I try to get as compact as possible and hold that position until I'm about to land. It makes grabbing easier and keeps my movement to a minimum."
>
> *Lucas Debari*

Tim Eddy looks over his shoulder to spot his landing on this backside 180 at Timberline, Oregon.

BACKSIDE 180s

Backside 180s are just like their frontside counterparts but turned in the opposite direction. You go through the same motion as when making a toeside turn, only you rotate the complete 180 degrees. Then you turn your body to face uphill and ride away backward (*switch*).

The backside 180 might just be the best trick in the book. It isn't that hard to execute, but once you feel what it's like to float blindly through the air, you'll know why so many snowboarders rank it as one of their favorite tricks.

The trick to doing backside 180s is trusting yourself and your ability. Practice them on flat ground first, then on any roller you can find around the mountain. When you feel confident, then apply what you've learned to the park.

As you ride up to the jump, make a *set-up turn* into a toeside turn. A set-up turn is simply a small heel- or toe-edge carve you use to get comfortable before you jump—basically just a way to situate yourself before the spin. Transfer your weight onto your toes as you start to head up the transition. Although you've made a minor carve into the jump, it's important to leave the lip like you would for a straight air, that is, flat-based. You don't want your board to be angled too steeply upward, as you could end up drifting too high and rotating into a 270.

As you pop off the lip, don't initiate any sort of spin. Just ollie and look uphill over your trailing shoulder. Turning your head will turn your body, and the rotation in the backside 180 is so minimal that it's easy to over-rotate. Just keep it simple and spin slowly.

It's best to first learn backside 180s without grabbing, but as you get more comfortable with the motion, try grabbing Indy, stalefish, or tail. Or just let your limbs hang—the back 180 is one trick that can look and feel just as cool without a grab.

Once you've turned about 90 degrees, start looking for the landing. It's easiest just to look down at your feet. It'll be kind of a blind landing, and you should not crane your neck to spot the transition because that would keep you rotating. Just look down at your board and you should see the landing starting to creep up.

A frontside grab during a frontside 360

Keep your knees sucked up and as you come around to fakie, extend your legs to land, but be careful not to straighten them completely. You don't want to land straight-legged, because you need to use your knees to absorb the landing. Make any last-minute adjustments so you can match your board to the transition and land flat-based. Absorb the landing with your knees and core, look forward, where you want to go, and ride away.

Landing switch is just like landing regular in that you'll want to absorb the landing with your lower body and core and keep your shoulders parallel to your board edges and your weight evenly distributed between your feet. Practice 180s on mellower slopes to get a feeling for landing switch, then when you're used to the feeling of coming down with your trailing foot leading, try taking it to a small park jump.

"It's easier when I'm coming around 90 to look at the landing and just stare at it until I land and then look up. That's always been how I do it."

Jordan Mendenhall

FRONTSIDE 360s

Frontside 360s (also called *frontside threes*) are one full rotation. You leave the lip, spin a full 360 degrees, and land riding in the original direction. Frontside 360s are pretty simple—some kids can learn them in the first week of riding—but to make them look pretty takes a good deal of practice.

First practice the rotation without leaving the snow. As you're riding downhill, initiate a heelside turn and skid it out 180 degrees. Then keep looking over your lead shoulder and rotate around another 180 degrees until you're faced downhill, riding the same way you were before, with your leading foot downhill.

Before trying the frontside three in the park, make sure you can do frontside 180s and threes on small jumps or even just on flat ground, to get a feel for the rotation and for landing flat-based. Then, when you feel totally comfortable, take them to the park jumps. Too often, beginning snowboarders try to force the frontside three, and it ends up looking really jerky. You want to spin smoothly, get a solid grab, stay compact, and ride away in a straight line, without carving too much.

For your first try in the terrain park, find a jump that you've hit a bunch and know the right speed for. You need to carry more speed than you'd want for a straight air, because you might end up scrubbing a little speed as you initiate your spin off the lip. Try doing a small set-up turn to help transfer your weight onto your heels. Just be careful to not overdo it and do a speed check instead. A *speed check* is basically a skidded turn that causes you to lose a lot of speed and momentum; this usually makes you come up short and land on the knuckle of the jump.

As you leave the lip, pop off your heels. Look back uphill over your leading shoulder while simultaneously sucking your knees up. Now go for a grab; frontside, mute, or melon are all grabs that come naturally on this trick. Hold your grab as long as possible, really concentrating on keeping your body quiet and compact.

When you rotate around to 270, look through your legs and try to spot your landing. At the same time, let go of your grab and prepare to put down your legs to absorb that landing.

Try to land either flat-based or a little on your toes. Do your best to avoid landing on your heels—with all the momentum you've got going, landing on your heel edge could make you wash out on your edge.

"The most important thing to remember when you're doing a frontside 360 is that you're going to be spinning blind for a moment. But if you started your spin smoothly, you'll come around and see your landing at the last minute. It'll be there. You just have to trust yourself and your ability, and not freak out."

Sean Genovese

BACKSIDE 360s

Like frontside 360s, backside 360s (also called *backside threes* or *back threes*) involve a complete rotation, only this time you're rotating backside, just like you do when you make a toeside turn. Backside 360s are a little easier than frontside 360s. Because the backside 360 isn't that intimidating a trick, it's one you can learn quickly and really have fun with. Like all the simple

spins in snowboarding, the backside 360 is a trick you could learn in a day but spend a lifetime perfecting.

Practice spinning on the snow first. Do a toeside turn, skid it out to a 180, and then keep looking over your trailing shoulder, letting your body follow until you've rotated around 360 degrees. Once you feel really comfortable doing backside 360s on snow, you have an understanding of your body positioning, and you could basically do them blindfolded, then you're ready to take them to a jump.

As you approach the lip, make a set-up turn and transfer your weight from your heels to your toes. Be careful not to carve too hard, as you don't want to lose speed. A back three doesn't involve a lot of rotation, so just ease into it as you head up the lip.

As you leave the lip, initiate the spin with your shoulders. As with any spin in snowboarding, you want to lead with your head. For the backside three, look over your back shoulder, essentially uphill. After you've left the lip, bring your knees up and reach for a grab.

A lot of different grabs come naturally when spinning a back three. Melon, Indy, and tail are all good choices, but really it's just a matter of doing what feels best at first. You can work toward what you think looks best later.

The most difficult part of this spin is the first 180 degrees. In that first half-rotation you need to be smooth; otherwise, the rest of the spin will be tough to bring around. When you get halfway through the rotation, start looking down at your board for the landing.

Always hold your grab as long as possible.

Once you get 270 degrees through your spin, let go of the grab and prepare to land. Keep your knees bent and be ready to absorb the landing with your lower body and core. Do your best to land flat-based and ride straight away.

"When you're bringing a backside 360 around, you want to make sure you hold your grab to at least 270 degrees. That'll help keep your body centered and set you up to land and stomp it."

Kimmy Fasani

FRONTSIDE 540s

A frontside 540 is simply a 360 plus a 180, or one and a half full rotations. Once you've figured out how to spin frontside 180s and 360s, you should be ready to put the two together and rotate a clean frontside 540. All the mechanics of this trick are the same as for the other frontside spins; if you're comfortable with those, you shouldn't have any problem with this one.

To practice, repeat the process of sliding on snow 360 degrees, but this time continue rotating another 180 degrees.

When you first try it at the park, approach the jump with more speed than you think you'll need. You'll inevitably scrub a little speed on your set-up turns or speed checks.

Ride toward the jump and, as you near the lip, make a set-up turn and transfer your weight onto your heels. As you did with the frontside three, make a mellow carve up the jump, always keeping your eye on the lip and being careful not to pre-spin too much. When spinning a 540, it's easy to get overly ambitious and try to force the spin too early. Be patient; you'll be airborne before you know it.

Wind up with your upper body; since you're going to be spinning frontside, rotate your shoulders and upper body in the other direction. Wait for that feeling of flight. As you leave the lip, start your spin with your head and shoulders. Bring your knees up, and lower your arms to grab your board. Try grabbing mute, melon, or stalefish. Keep your body compact, and keep looking over your leading shoulder.

As you come around to 360 degrees, let go of the grab and start opening up your upper body and lowering your legs. Take a half-second to spot the landing and make any last-minute adjustments. It can be easy to lean a little too far back when you spin a 540, so you might have to correct your body positioning. Concentrate on getting your board parallel to the landing. Lower your legs, stomping square on both feet and putting equal pressure on both legs. Do your best to land with a flat base and ride away fakie.

"Sometimes with frontside fives, it can be easy to get a little *corked out*, or inverted, in the air. If that happens to you, don't get freaked out. It's okay—you'll come around onto your feet. Just keep your upper body composed and stay confident in your ability—that's the most important thing."

Jordan Mendenhall

BACKSIDE 540s

A backside 540 is simply a backside 360 combined with a backside 180. Rare is the spin that's thrown as frequently as the back five. Just watch the local park jump line any given Saturday, and you'll see that a backside five is indeed a must-have.

Before you go throwing backside 540s, make sure you have both backside 360s and backside 180s completely figured. Once you're comfortable spinning backside and landing switch, then give the backside 540 a try. To practice these on the snow, slide around on your toe edge one and a half rotations.

Here's how to do your first one on a jump: As you approach the jump, make a set-up turn. Then, when you're riding up the lip, initiate a mellow toeside turn and transfer your weight onto your toes. At this point, you also want to wind up your shoulders a little. Basically, open your upper body in the opposite direction from the way you're going to spin. That way, when you leave the lip, you have a little more torque (force causing you to rotate).

Right before your board leaves the lip, counter-rotate with your upper body. Then as you leave the lip, pop off your toes and initiate the spin with your arms, shoulders, and head by throwing them in the direction you want to spin—backside. Bring your knees up and reach down to grab. With a backside five, the easiest grabs are the melon, Indy, and tail. Try to get your grab as early as possible; it helps you stay compact and lets you spin that much faster. Once you're grabbing, just keep looking over your trailing shoulder.

As you come around to 360 degrees, take a quick look at the landing to make sure you'll make it to the sweet spot in the transition. It's easy to get off-balance when spinning a 540. Usually people lean too far back and land on the nose of their board. Keep your shoulders parallel to the deck while you're rotating and you shouldn't have any problem staying upright. The last 180 degrees of rotation is the time to make any necessary adjustments.

Once you get to 450 degrees, let go of your grab, lower your legs a little, and prepare to land flat-based. The last part of this trick will feel a lot like a backside 180, so be ready for that sensation of flying blind. Concentrate on looking down at your board to spot the landing and trust yourself.

"If you know how to do backside threes, all you have to do is pop a little bit harder to do a backside five. You also want to throw a little bit more spin off the lip. Basically, all the work is actually on the lip, so that's the main thing you want to focus on."

Eero Ettala

PARK RAILS

Rails are intimidating. They're cold, hard, and easy to fall on. But approach rail riding with the right mindset and even the most fundamental understanding of the skills needed, and you'll find that rails aren't as scary as they might seem. Once you get a feel for sliding on steel, it's easy to take what you've learned on the smaller rails and apply it to longer, steeper, and more technical rails. Next time you're at the mountain, notice how many kids are sessioning all the different rail features. Rails are popular for a reason; they're challenging, but it's easy to progress on them in a short time.

That being said, try the fun boxes before you go jumping on every rail in the park. Fun boxes are a great place to learn to slide flat-based. They provide a bigger surface

A downrail is any rail set up on a downhill angle on the slope.

for you to balance on, and they're typically set up closer to the snow and in more beginner-friendly angles. And, as the name implies, they're really fun. You can see anyone from first-timers to seasoned vets sliding their days away on these boxes, and you should follow their lead. In the following section, the term *rail* is used for whatever feature you're riding, but do learn all these tricks on a fun box first, before taking them to the rails.

50-50s

In a *50-50*, your board slides in line with the rail, that is, your edges are parallel to the rail. The 50-50 is the foundation for all rail tricks. It's the easiest trick to learn and allows a lot of room for error. The beauty of the 50-50 is that if you jump on the rail and feel uncertain, you simply jump right back off. The body positioning is pretty much the same as when you ride down the mountain, so all you have to do is get used to balancing on a plastic box or steel rail.

The first step is learning to ollie onto the rail. All rails should be built with a lip that you can pop off of. You can either ollie on backside, facing away from the rail, or frontside, facing the rail.

Jumping on frontside is easier and

50-50s are the best starting point when learning rail tricks.

should be the first way you try. Ride up to the rail at a slight angle—not too much, as you don't want your momentum to carry you over and off the other side of the rail. You want to be angled pretty much parallel to the rail. Pick a spot a foot or two down the rail and aim to land on that spot. Ollieing up backside is basically the same; the only difference is you're coming in on your heel edge.

Ollie up onto the rail. Don't ollie too high, because then you'll come down onto the rail with too much force. Jump just high enough to get on the rail. When you land on the rail, keep your knees bent and, as with any landing, try to absorb the impact with your knees and core. Use your arms for balance and lock into your 50-50.

Keep equal pressure on both legs, and concentrate on staying centered and balanced on the rail. As with any trick in snowboarding, it's always best to look in the direction you want to go. Stare at the end of the rail. Your board will follow your body, which will follow your eyes, so look toward the end of the rail until you reach it, then look at the landing.

Ride off the end of the rail, landing with your knees bent and your board flat-based. Ride away, and repeat the whole process on the next rail or box.

Stay low and use your arms for balance when doing boardslides.

"The most important thing with 50-50s is to focus on keeping your board headed straight down the rail. Keep your knees bent, stay low and, if you remember to always look at the end of the rail, that's where you'll go."

J.P. Walker

BOARDSLIDES

Boardslides require a good deal of balance. As with all these rail tricks, the boardslide is best learned on a small fun box that is close to the ground and has little to no angle. A wide sliding surface makes it that much easier to get a feel for it. Before you start on boardslides, make sure you can pop frontside 180s and ride away fakie comfortably.

The most important thing to remember when learning boardslides is to slide completely flat-based. It's a hard feeling to figure out at first, because the tendency in snowboarding is to be on one edge or the other. But when trying boardslides, if you lean too far forward, you'll inevitably catch your toe edge and fall on your face; lean too far back and you'll slip out and land on your back or butt.

Approach the rail at a slight angle, from the right if you're regular, or from the left if you're goofy. Pop off the lip with enough speed to get up onto the rail.

Keep the rail between your bindings on frontside boardslides.

Land on the rail, making sure your board is *flush* or flat against it. If the rail is on an angle, you need to lean farther forward than you might think. Keep your hands in front of you and your knees bent for balance.

Once you're sliding, concentrate on the end of the rail. Keep the rail centered between your bindings and your base flat all the way down the rail. Stay low with your knees bent and your upper body quiet, using your arms for balance.

At the end of the rail, turn your shoulders slightly, bringing your board either back to regular or around to fakie. You don't need to jump off the end of the rail; just suck your knees up a little and spot the landing. Make sure to get your rotation around quickly enough to avoid the dreaded toe-edge catch when you're coming off the rail. Stomp flat-based, with equal pressure on both feet, and ride away.

"You want to be comfortable doing frontside 180s, because the movement in a boardslide is basically the same as in a frontside 180. So try to do little 180s off moguls and maybe even next to the rail to get comfortable with that motion."

Leanne Pelosi

FRONTSIDE BOARDSLIDES

There are few tricks as stylish as the frontside boardslide. This challenging trick can take years to master, but with an understanding of the basic body position and a good deal of commitment, you can learn to do it.

Try frontside boardslides first on a fun box, then move on to a small down rail, nothing with too aggressive an ollie. You have to lean downhill more than might feel natural. Learning frontsides is a mental battle, because you need to slide blind and backward. Don't let that deter you. Once you figure it out and learn to get your board flat-based, you'll find that frontsides are one of the coolest-feeling rail tricks.

Approach the rail at a bit of an angle, just a little off parallel. Come at the rail from the left if you ride regular, from the right if you're a goofy-footer. Line up a little bit away from the rail, so you have room to pop up and onto the rail without catching the nose of your board. Pick a spot a couple feet down the rail to aim to put your board on.

Ollie just high enough to sneak your board's nose up and onto the rail. As you ollie, turn your shoulders perpendicular to the rail, looking at the spot on the rail where you're going to first make contact.

As your board finds the rail, make sure it's flat-based. Keep your lower body loose and your knees ready to make any last-minute adjustments. When you're first learning this trick, it's easiest to keep the rail under your front foot. This allows you to jump off the rail if you get off-balance. As you learn the frontside, try to slide with the rail under the middle of your board, between your bindings.

Once you're locked in, look over your leading shoulder at the end of the rail. You'll really have to crane your neck, but this body position helps keep you centered on the rail and allows you to see where you're going. Also, when you come off, it makes it easier to ride away regular.

As you near the end of the rail, turn your shoulders back downhill. Your lower body and board will follow, and you'll ride away regular. As always, stomp square on both feet, with equal pressure on both legs and your board flat-based.

"The frontside broadslide is one of the most basic tricks in snowboarding, but to do it properly is the tough part. You can learn it a certain way, like on your foot, or not turned all the way, but the biggest trick is to do them every day so you can do it completely proper—that is, turn it completely 90—and slide with the rail right in between your bindings."

Nima Jalali

NOSE PRESSES

Nose presses are essentially just 50-50s with a little more lean. The fundamentals of the

Put all your weight on the nose of your board to get it to press properly on a fun box.

two tricks are the same, but with the nose press you lean all your weight on your front leg and balance on the nose of your board. The best way to figure out how to do nose presses is to try them on the snow first. Pop a little ollie, land on your front foot, and really lean into it.

Once you're comfortable pressing your board, find a small fun box that's set up with little to no angle. Practice a few 50-50s, and, at the end of the slide, exaggerate your lean a little to get a feel for it.

When you're ready, approach the box at a slight angle, with enough speed to crack an ollie up and onto the box. As with the 50-50,

you want to approach the box frontside—from the left if you ride regular, and from the right if you're a goofy-footer.

Keep your shoulders parallel to the box and really lean into the press. You have to commit to keeping your tail up, which probably means leaning into it more than you would think. Try straightening your back leg while you're pressing, and keep your eyes on the end of the box.

Once you get to the end, pop a little ollie out of your press and suck your knees up to your chest, making sure to keep your tail up so it doesn't tap the end of the box. Giving the landing a quick look, stomp down on both feet and flat-based.

When you feel comfortable jumping on frontside, try the nose press backside, that is, ollieing on from the other side. Again, use all the techniques you learned for ollieing on frontside and apply them to the backside ollie. Come in at a slight angle, stay low, and focus on the box. Once you leave the lip, ollie just high enough to get onto the box and then stay centered with your knees bent.

Once you feel really comfortable on fun boxes of every shape and size then you should be ready to take these tricks to the rails.

"Once you get into your press, really bend your front leg and straighten your back leg. It's going to take you a little while to figure out where your weight needs to be to balance on a nose press, but do enough of them and you'll figure it out."

Stevie Bell

TAIL PRESSES

Tail presses. Tail wheelies. Five-0s. This maneuver has a lot of names, but the trick remains the same. Like nose presses, tail presses are fundamentally similar to 50-50s. You want to keep your shoulders parallel to the box and keep the box centered in the middle of your board.

To get the feeling of tail presses, try doing little ollies and tail presses on the snow. This will give you an idea of how to flex your board and hold that press. When you feel comfortable popping an ollie into a press, try it on a fun box that's set up flat or at a slight angle.

Approach the box from the left if you're regular or from the right if you're a goofy-footer. Don't pop too big of an ollie to get into your tail press. If you ollie too aggressively, you might end up just tapping your tail rather than pressing it. A smaller ollie will help you lay into a solid tail press.

Once you're on the box and locked into the press, put all your weight on your back leg. Straightening your front leg will help you keep it pressed.

Keep your shoulders parallel to the box while you're sliding. This helps you avoid letting your board drift or veer in one direction or the other. Keep the box centered under your board, with your board pointed straight ahead, and always look at the end of the box.

Once you get to the end, pop a little bit and bring your knees up, getting ready to absorb that landing with your legs and core. Land flat-based.

"The way to make it look legit is to hold it the whole way through and just put all that pressure on your back foot—that should help you keep the tail press up all the way through the rail."

Darrel Mathes

Put a lot of weight on your back leg when doing tail presses.

BASIC PARK ETIQUETTE

Wait your turn at every feature.

Call your drop in. Let other riders know you're going.

Always give the downhill rider the right-of-way.

Don't stand or sit on jumps.

Don't stand or sit on landings.

Don't stand or sit in any area of high traffic.

If you fall, get out of the way as quickly as possible.

Always be alert and aware of your surroundings.

If there's a crowd when you roll up to the park, make sure you wait your turn and call your drop.

CHAPTER 5

Throwing down in the Breckenridge Superpipe

Pipe Riding

Although most beginners can find their way to and down a half-pipe, when it comes to riding the pipe there's really nothing beginner about it. To ride a half-pipe well takes a lot of practice, which might be why half-pipes seem to be getting less and less attention from fledgling shreds these days. Sure, half-pipes draw crowds of spectators at events like the Winter X-Games and the Olympics, but check out the pipe at your local resort on any given Sunday. Odds are not nearly as many kids are hiking it as are lapping the jumps, rails, and boxes. Learning to ride pipe requires a lot of dedication, and a good deal of hiking too. But don't let that discourage you from trying, because you're sure to find that the sensation of blasting out of the half-pipe is like nothing else on a snowboard. The bottom line is that with pipe riding, the reward greatly outweighs all the hard work.

For those who might have a hard time picturing what a pipe run looks like, here's a simplified breakdown of how it should play out. You start just uphill of the pipe and decide which wall of the pipe you want to drop in on. Ride down along the wall, parallel to the lip of the pipe. When you're going as fast as you can while still feeling in control, you turn your board toward the pipe and drop down the wall. You cut across the bottom of the half-pipe (called the *flatbottom*) and head straight up the other wall. With enough speed you can make it up and out of the lip (called a hit or *airing out*). Turning or spinning your board and body around, you land back on the same transition and ride toward the other wall. And that's all you do: ride back and forth down the pipe, ideally pushing yourself to go faster and higher with every hit. You can expect to get between six and ten hits per pipe run. When you make it to the bottom of the pipe you can either ride the lift up and lap it, or unstrap your board from your feet, hike back up to the top, and do it all again.

The skills you need in the pipe are fundamentally the same as in the park. A lot of the moves are the same. You always want to look in the direction you want to go, keep your upper body quiet and compact, and be in that "ready" position with your knees bent and your arms just out in front of you for balance.

That being said, there are major differences between park riding and pipe riding. Pipe riding requires a great deal of edge control. Since the pipe is pretty much one giant section of transition, you're almost constantly transferring from one edge to the other. Most serious pipe riders sharpen their edges regularly. If you plan on riding a lot of pipe, you might consider it as well. (See the "Snowboard Prep and Repair" section in Chapter 6.) Sharp edges will help you in the pipe.

A healthy amount of bravado can't hurt either, as half-pipe riding requires a lot of speed. With the 18- to 22-foot walls of today's half-pipes, commonly called Superpipes, you've got to really haul carcass to make it all the way to the top of the wall, let alone jump out of it.

The sheer size of these Superpipes is intimidating, and it's easy for beginners to dismiss the pipe as being too difficult or too dangerous, but once you try riding a half-pipe you'll quickly see how safe it is and also how much room for progression it offers.

UNDERSTANDING TRANSITION

Thanks to transition, today's half-pipes are not too difficult or too dangerous for beginner or intermediate snowboarders. Again, transitions, or tranny, are the places where the snow is angled perfectly for a smooth landing. When jumping, you want to take off from transition and land on transition. And since the half-pipe is pretty much all transition, it's a great place to get some air, right? Yes, it is.

The beauty of the longer, more mellow transitions found in Superpipes is that they allow a lot of room for error. Whether you're making it halfway up the wall, just barely making it out, or catching a couple feet of air, if anything goes wrong you've got 18-plus feet of tranny to land in. It's good to remind yourself of this every time you drop into the pipe. It should help you approach those walls with more and more speed every time.

UNDERSTANDING HALF-PIPE DESIGN

Half-pipe design has come a long way in the last twenty years. The first half-pipes were dug by hand by the snowboarders who would be riding them. Those early pipes were understandably crude replicas of the half-pipes used by skateboarders. The walls were much shorter than those on today's Superpipes and, because they were built by hand (and shovel), the transitions weren't all that smooth—which is a nice way of saying they were pretty rough.

Early pipes laid the groundwork, though, and in the 1990s a machine called a "Pipe Dragon" revolutionized their design. The Pipe Dragon could cut uniform transition. For the first time, the same pipe could be built twice, and once built it could be maintained for an entire season. The Pipe Dragon remained the paradigm for a while, but eventually snowboarders began pushing the limits of the 12-foot walls the Dragon

The 22-foot X-Games Superpipe

cut. Before long, their riding demanded a bigger and better pipe.

And then the Zaugg was born. This new machine could cut a pipe with 16- or 18-foot walls, depending on the model. Today there's a Zaugg that cuts 22-foot pipe walls, which is the Olympic standard. Resorts spend hundreds of thousands of dollars building and maintaining their half-pipes, and they often employ a snowcat driver dedicated specifically to building and cutting the pipe. The result of all these advances in design and maintenance are better-built half-pipes that are easier to ride and subsequently easier to progress in.

UNDERSTANDING SNOW CONDITIONS

Your success in the pipe is largely dependent on the condition of the snow in that pipe. If it's bitter cold and the pipe is a sheet of ice, odds are you're going to have a

Check the condition of the snow in the pipe before you drop and you'll save yourself a few falls.

hell of a time getting the edge of your board to hold, so you'll struggle with navigating the transition—not to mention the fear and resultant timidity that icy conditions inspire. However, if it's too warm and the pipe is slushy and soft, you could have a hard time keeping your speed and will find you can't even make it up the walls, let alone out.

There's no formula for the perfect conditions for pipe riding. Everyone's opinion of what's ideal is different. Some say a harder, almost icy wall is better, while others prefer a softer, semi-slushy wall. You need to figure out what you're most comfortable riding. Ride as much pipe as possible, figure out all the differences in all the conditions, determine when you feel most confident, and ride as much as you can on those days.

PREPPING YOUR BOARD

Properly tuning your board for the half-pipe can also play a huge role in your success. You want to make sure your board is waxed and the edges are sharp, so you can generate the speed you need and hold your line up the walls. See Chapter 6 for tips on tuning and waxing your board.

DROPPING IN AND AIRING OUT

The first thing to do is to figure out your drop-in. The *drop-in* is when you first enter the pipe. Ride up to the wall opposite the one that you plan on airing out of. Ride parallel to

Dropping into the pipe at Breckenridge, Colorado

that wall for a second, and then roll over the lip. Turn your board perpendicular to the lip, tuck your knees up, and drop into the pipe, catching as much transition as possible. Then point your board straight at the opposite wall.

When it comes to *airing out*, or catching air out of the half-pipe, approach it a lot like you would any park jump. Although pipe riding requires using your edges a lot more, you don't want to be on edge when you take off from the wall. It's important to use your edges as you approach the lip of the pipe, but you want to be flat-based when you pop off the lip. If you have too much weight on your edge, you won't have enough speed to get air and you might fly into the air off-balance.

The success of your first hit, and really the rest of your pipe run, hinges on your drop-in. To learn how to drop in, it helps to watch the riders who are really ripping. Notice where they drop in and follow their lines. You can probably see their tracks in the pipe. If it looks like they know what they're doing, try to imitate them.

PIPE TRICKS

The key to learning any pipe trick is speed. You have to ride fast in the pipe, and the best way to keep your speed is edge control. It's important to use your edges to hold your line in the pipe. After you drop in, you want to ride straight at the next wall without making any turns. The sooner you can feel comfortable on edge and holding your lines in the pipe, the sooner you'll be blasting airs up and out of the lip.

The beauty of the half-pipe is that it's easy to start small and work your way up. Take your time getting a sense of how the pipe rides. Get confident riding back and forth through the transition. Once you're comfortable simply riding the wall, try doing small ollies at the peak of your line up each wall. You'll naturally feel unweighted at this point in the wall, so an ollie should come easily. When you do these little airs, turn your board back into the pipe. Even though you're turning a little, that's considered a straight air in the pipe. If you do one on your frontside wall (the wall you ride up on your toes), that's called a frontside air.

And if you do one on your backside wall (the wall you ride up on your heels), that's a backside air. That's a good place to start.

BACKSIDE AIRS

As you now know, a *backside air* is basically a straight air or ollie performed on the backside wall of the half-pipe. The backside wall is the one that you approach on your heel edge. More specifically, it's the left wall if you ride regular and the right wall if you ride goofy.

Although some people find them intimidating, backside airs are easy to really boost once you know how to approach the backside wall on your heel edge. It all starts with the drop-in. Drop at the top of your frontside wall. Stay low and compact through the transition, and carry as much speed as you can across the flat-bottom.

As you start up the backside wall, transfer some of your weight onto your back leg and start looking up and out of the pipe. Remember, if you concentrate on the lip, that's probably as high as you'll get, so aim for the sky. Look out of the pipe and stay compact as you travel up the wall.

Once you're at the lip, stand up a little, but don't pop like you would on a park jump. The half-pipe is designed to do most of the work for you, so let the pipe shoot you up and out. Once you're in the air, suck your knees up and grab Indy or melon or maybe tail—they should all be pretty easy for backside airs. Hold your grab as long as possible. This keeps your body quiet and compact, and also makes your air look that much more stylish.

Aspire to blast backside airs this big someday, but for now start small and work your way up.

When you've reached the top of your trajectory, start looking back down in the pipe. As you descend, pay attention to where you're going to land and adjust your legs accordingly. Try to land at the top of the transition just slightly on your toe edge with your knees bent. It's always good to land higher on the tranny so you have a lot of speed to carry you through the transition, across the flat-bottom and into the frontside wall.

Remember: More speed equals more airtime in the pipe, so keep hiking higher for your drop, going faster through the transition, and pushing yourself harder with every run.

> "It helps to have some forward lean on your bindings for backside airs. The more forward lean you have, the more control you have on your heels, because you have to do less work with your legs. With forward lean, the binding will do more work for you."
>
> *Chad Otterstrom*

Grabbing melon comes naturally when doing frontside airs.

FRONTSIDE AIRS

Frontside airs are just like backside airs except performed on the frontside wall. The frontside wall is the one you approach on your toe edge. It is the right wall if you ride regular or the left wall if you ride goofy.

Frontside airs are typically less intimidating than backside airs, but they actually require a little more skill. Sometimes when you're trying to do a frontside air, it's easy to take too aggressive a line up the wall. If you go too straight up the wall, you can lose all your speed and have trouble getting out of the lip. It's a good idea for beginners to watch the line that other riders are taking and follow their lead.

Make a good drop-in, and stay low and compact through the transition. Transfer from your toe edge to flat-based through the flat-bottom and really charge into the frontside wall. The more speed you can carry into the wall the better, because you'll inevitably lose some speed as you ride up the pipe wall. You want to be slightly on your toe edge as you head toward the top of the wall, and then flat-based as you're leaving the lip. Don't overthink it. Just concentrate on keeping your speed and staying low.

As you near the top of the wall, concentrate on looking above the lip. You only go as high as you look, so focus on a point above the lip. Then let the pipe do the work, stay relaxed, and get ready for some airtime.

Once you leave the lip, turn your upper body slightly, initiating the rotation with your head. Look where you want to go, which is back into the pipe. It's easy to over-rotate a frontside air. The rotation should be minimal. Grabbing nose will help limit your rotation, but stalefish and tail-grabs are also good options. Do what feels most natural.

Keep your knees sucked up and your body quiet, and look at where you want to land. Try to land flat-based as high on the transition as possible. Keep your body compact and carry all your speed down the tranny, into the flat-bottom and across to the next hit.

"Don't try and go super-high on your first try; just keep it mellow. It's really fun to just grab your nose and put your tail on the lip. So try that a couple of times and then just start carrying more and more speed into it. You've got to practice to get up there, that's for sure."

Hampus Mosesson

AIR-TO-FAKIES

After you've figured out the fundamentals of straight airs, learning air-to-fakies should be your next step. Air-to-fakies are almost easier than frontside and backside airs because they require almost no rotation.

Tail grabs help keep your upper body quiet when doing air-to-fakies.

What's key is feeling comfortable riding switch. Also, make sure you've got backside 180s down before you try air-to-fakies.

Air-to-fakies are typically easier to do on your frontside wall. Once you feel ready to give air-to-fakies a try, approach the frontside wall the same way you would when doing a frontside air. Drop in with confidence, then stay low and centered over your board through the transition. Begin to stand up a little as you start climbing the frontside wall.

Heading toward the lip, keep your weight slightly over your toe edge so you can hold a good line up the frontside wall. An air-to-fakie feels similar to a backside 180 on a park jump, so expect that feeling of flying semi-blind.

As you're about to leave the lip, concentrate on looking up and out of the pipe. Take off the same way you would for a straight air. Let the pipe wall do the work. Don't pop, just stay low and keep your upper body quiet. When you leave the lip, don't turn your head or shoulders down the pipe as you would for a straight air. Instead, just float there.

Now go for a grab. Tail, Indy, or melon grabs should come easy. You won't really be able to spot your landing, so watch the lip underneath you. As you're coming back into the tranny, extend your legs to meet the snow and be ready to make any necessary adjustments.

Try to touch down as high on the wall as possible. Land flat-based and with your weight centered over your board. As you're riding down the transition and toward the backside wall, transfer your weight back onto your toe edge and start looking toward the backside wall for your next hit.

Try grabbing frontside—anywhere along your toe edge—when doing frontside 360s in the pipe.

"Landing an air-to-fakie is pretty tricky because you can't really see your landing. You just have to trust yourself and trust your pop and feel it out. Take it slow in the beginning and work your way up, and just have fun with it."

Markku Koski

FRONTSIDE 360s

The beauty of spinning in the half-pipe is that you aren't really doing the full rotation. Since you're initiating and completing your rotation at a slight angle, you're not completing the entire spin. But that doesn't necessarily make these maneuvers any easier.

Spinning in the pipe is tricky. Get overzealous and you might end up hucking yourself into the flat-bottom. But if you don't spin hard enough, you could catch an edge on the pipe wall and, again, find yourself on the bottom of the pipe. Remember, today's half-pipes are built with a lot of transition. Even if you do miscalculate your spin and lose it in the air, at least you've got a lot of room for error.

The first step toward learning 360s in the pipe is to make sure you can do frontside 180s and 360s on flat ground and on small jumps. You need to really understand how to rotate and land flat-based before you start spinning in the half-pipe.

Frontside 360s are best learned on the frontside wall. Keep in mind that this trick is really just an over-rotated frontside air. Also, you ride away from this trick fakie, so learning air-to-fakies first is crucial.

Drop in on the pipe from the backside wall. Stay centered over your board, and pick a line up the frontside wall that you feel comfortable with. Don't expect to boost out of the pipe on your first attempt. Like any pipe trick, frontside 360s can be done below the lip.

As you start up the wall, make sure you're flat-based. If you use your edges too much, you'll have an even harder time trying to spin. Trust the design of the pipe.

When you leave the lip, pop slightly off your heels and look down into the pipe over your leading shoulder. Simultaneously, suck your knees up so you can get a grab. Mute, melon, and stalefish are all grabs that should come naturally.

Holding your grab as long as possible, spot your landing. You can see everything that's going on while you're doing a frontside 360, so take it all in. Notice where you are in relation to the lip, and anticipate where you might land in the transition. Also concentrate on keeping your body quiet and compact.

When coming back into the pipe, lower your legs and prepare to ride away fakie. Try to land as close to the top of the transition as possible and with your weight a little on your toes. This helps you keep your edge and your speed for the next hit.

Try grabbing melon on backside 360s.

"In my opinion, frontside 360s are 100 percent about committing with your shoulders. When you open your shoulders toward the center of the pipe, your feet will automatically follow the movement of your shoulders, seeing as how they are connected by your spine and that's connected to your lower body."

Ryan Thompson

BACKSIDE 360s

Back threes are more challenging than frontside 360s in the pipe because you have to rotate blindly. A backside three doesn't require much more rotation than a backside air, but that extra little bit of spinning can be tough to master because you can't really see where you're going.

This is one trick that you should definitely practice a lot in the park and on flat ground before you take it to the pipe. And then once you do decide to try spinning backside in the pipe, start small and try it below the lip.

Just like on the frontside 360, you ride away from this trick fakie, so make sure you feel comfortable riding down the backside wall on your heel edge. Try a few air-to-fakies on this wall to get a feel for riding away from the lip fakie.

When you feel confident, drop in on the

frontside wall. Stay low and compact, keeping your weight centered over your board. As you ride through the flat-bottom and up the backside wall, you want to be flat-based. Start eyeing the lip of the pipe and transferring some of your weight over your back foot.

Choose a line up the wall that isn't too steep and won't carry you too far down the pipe. Again, it helps to pay close attention to riders in the pipe who seem to know what they're doing. Study their every move, especially on the backside wall.

Carry as much speed as you can into the backside wall. As your front foot leaves the lip, initiate the spin with your head and shoulders by looking back over your trailing arm and down into the pipe.

Suck your knees up to your chest and grab. Grabbing backside, Indy or tail should be easiest. After you've rotated past 180 degrees, keep looking over your back shoulder and finish the rotation. This is probably the scariest part of the trick, since you can't see the pipe or where you'll land.

Trust yourself and your understanding of the transition. As you're about to land, notice how your body is oriented in the air and make any adjustments necessary to ensure that you land flat on the base of your board. It's really important to land flat-based on the backside 360, because landing with too much weight on your heels will most likely cause you to slide out.

After you touch down, make sure to look down the pipe, across the flat-bottom, and up at the next hit on the frontside wall. Again, a lot of practice riding fakie will help with this.

"For a 360 on the backside wall, remember to wait until after you've left the lip to start your spin. If you spin too early, you're going to catch your heel edge."

Sean Genovese

FRONTSIDE 540s

Having figured out how to do straight airs, air-to-fakies, and both frontside and backside 360s, it's time for you to put everything you've learned together and try a 540 (also called a *five*).

Being proficient at the angled takeoff and landing of all pipe tricks will help you make a 540. If you feel really comfortable doing frontside 360s in the park, then you shouldn't have a problem with fives. Convincing yourself of this is the first step when it comes to trying this trick. Confidence is a huge part of snowboarding, and it really proves the old adage that you can do anything you put your mind to.

Some might argue that the frontside 540 is easier than a frontside 360 in the pipe because you ride away from it regular, rather than fakie. But don't try to skip steps and jump right into doing fives. As with every trick you learn in snowboarding, it's important to start small and work your way up. Get the fundamentals figured out, then put all the pieces together and go for it. For the five, you want to make sure you've got frontside straight airs and frontside 360s dialed in. Once you feel comfortable with both frontside straight airs and frontside

360s, all you have to do is put the two tricks together.

Drop in on the backside wall and carry as much speed as you can muster across the flat-bottom and up the frontside wall. As you head up the wall, center your weight over your board and flatten out your base.

In order to get your rotation around one and a half times, you need to initiate a powerful spin. So, as with any frontside spin on a jump, you want to counter-rotate, or wind up your upper body just before you leave the lip of the pipe. Concentrate on looking out of the pipe and try not to start your spin too early.

When your board leaves the lip, initiate the spin with your head and shoulders. Let the pipe wall shoot you up and out. As you're spinning, keep looking over your leading shoulder. Keep your shoulders flat, or parallel to your snowboard. This makes landing a lot easier, as you won't have to correct much when you're coming into the landing. Keep your shoulders parallel to your board and you'll stay compact, centered and composed in the air. When spinning in the half-pipe, it's easy to get off-axis, meaning that your board is rotating on a different plane than the deck of the pipe, but if you concentrate on keeping your shoulders and your board parallel, you can avoid getting off-kilter in the air.

Grab your board as soon as you've left the lip. Grabbing early and holding on as long as possible helps you get your rotation around. Mute, melon, or stalefish should come easiest.

Once you've rotated around 360 degrees, the hard part is over. All you have to do is

Grabbing tail while spinning frontside 540s helps to keep you on axis.

keep looking over your shoulder and down into the pipe. Let go of the grab, spot your landing, and prepare to put your board down flat-based. It's easy to land with your weight on your heels, but that will often cause you to slide out or lose your edge. After you've landed, stay low and compact. Point it into the next hit on the backside wall.

"For any frontside spins, you should always keep your shoulders super flat and instead of dropping your shoulder, tuck your head into your front shoulder. It'll keep your board flat and make it easier to spot your landing."

Bryan Fox

BACKSIDE 540s

Backside fives are easier to do in the half-pipe than on park jumps. Although they might seem like a really intimidating trick to try in the pipe, you shouldn't have any problem as long as you learn them in the park first and then apply what you know to the pipe. Like the frontside 540, the backside 540 is essentially a 360 plus a backside air. And since the hardest part of that equation is the first 360 degrees of rotation, once you have the backside three figured out, you're well on your way. Think about it: Once you get to that point in the spin, all you have to do is turn down another backside air, and since you can see everything in front of you, it should be as easy as that.

Again, pick a line up the wall that isn't too steep and won't carry you too far down the wall. Practice fives below the lip until you're completely comfortable with the rotation. Then commit to making it out of the pipe, and come in with as much speed as you can handle. You want to be on your heelside edge while you're dropping in, but when you're crossing the flat-bottom and going up into the backside wall, start trans-fering to a flat-based board position.

As you approach the lip, counter-rotate your shoulders. When your back foot is at the lip, initiate the spin with your upper body. Your body will follow your head, so keep looking over your trailing shoulder and your rotation will come around. Really throw your leading arm back toward your back leg and down into the pipe. As you do this, reach for your grab. Mute or melon should work best.

Once you're a little more than 360 degrees through your rotation, you can see the transition and adjust for your landing. Hold the grab as long as possible—both for style points and to keep your body compact—and continue to rotate. After you've come around a full 360 degrees and can see your landing, open your upper body to slow your spin. Spot your landing, and adjust your lower half so you land as high up on the transition as possible.

Land square on both feet and mostly flat-based, or slightly on your toe edge. Once you're riding down the transition, look up and across the pipe, toward the next hit on the frontside wall.

"If the pipe wall is a little verty, definitely don't use any pop whatsoever; otherwise, you'll be hurting. Ride off the lip smoothly, just like you would if you were riding off a jump, except that there's a bit more transition."

Steve Fischer

Throwing a backside 540 with a melon grab at Park City, Utah

A textbook Andrecht at Mount Hood, Oregon

HANDPLANTS

Handplants (also called *inverts*) might not seem like something the beginner or intermediate snowboarder could handle, but in reality they are more finesse moves than anything. It doesn't take herculean strength to put a hand down on the lip and briefly support yourself on it. You just need an understanding of transition and a commitment to getting inverted.

Wide varieties of handplants have been invented, so every snowboarder should have at least one in his or her bag of tricks. *Andrechts* are probably the best plants to learn first. To do an Andrecht, plant your trailing hand and grab your board with your leading hand. Like all handplants, they are more about timing than brute strength. Riders of smaller statures or less-than-impressive bicep circumferences have no excuse for not learning how to do handplants.

Handplants are easiest to learn on a quarter-pipe. A quarter-pipe is essentially just one wall of a halfpipe that isn't angled downhill like a half-pipe. Quarter-pipes are easier to learn handplants on because you can come at the lip flat-based, as opposed to a half-pipe, where you're bound to be on an edge due to the slope of the pipe. If your local resort has a quarter-pipe, go there first. If not, head to the bottom of the pipe or to the last 50 feet or so, where the pipe walls typically taper off a little. This section of the pipe is best for learning handplants because there's usually less vert on the walls and it's easy to hike over and over again.

You can do Andrechts on either wall of the pipe. The motions for this handplant are really similar to the motions for a small backside air. Try an Andrecht on the backside wall first, and if that doesn't seem to work, try them on the frontside wall.

Come at the wall with enough speed to do a small backside air. Approaching the lip, start transferring your weight onto your back foot. As you leave the lip, pop a little and put your hand down where your board just left the snow. It's crucial to stay low as you're riding up the wall. You can almost drag your backhand and, just as your board leaves the lip, plant your hand on the snow and kick your lower body up. The motion is similar to doing a cartwheel.

When you plant your hand, look down into the transition. If you're looking at the deck, you'll probably flop onto it, so concentrate on staring down the transition into the pipe.

While you're inverted, keep your knees tucked up to your chest and go for a grab. A melon grab is probably the easiest. Getting a good grab makes it much easier to bring yourself back into the transition. The more compact you keep your body, the easier it'll be to do a handplant.

Stay compact until your board is back on the snow. Land flat-based with your weight centered over both feet. Then slowly stand up as you're riding down the wall and into the flat-bottom.

"The mistake people make is they lunge forward and reach out for the deck or the coping (lip). You want to do a kind of reverse cartwheel and put your hand down right where you took off or as close to your tail as possible."

J.P. Walker

CHAPTER 6

Terrain with a lot of rocks is sure to take a toll on your board. Learn to repair damage yourself to keep your board looking and riding like new.

Caring for Your Equipment

Snowboard equipment is easy to neglect. You get home after a long, cold day on the hill and all you want to do is peel all that wet gear off and settle in for the night. But leave your outerwear in a pile, your board outside, or your boots in the garage, and the next day won't be nearly as pleasant. Your pants and jacket will be soggy and cold; your board's base will be dried out and the edges rusted; and your boots will probably smell like a wet dog, not to mention being cold and clammy. Keep up this habit all season, and all that gear you spent your hard-earned money on is liable to be ruined. Moral of the story: Take care of your gear and it'll take care of you.

Take small steps to care for your gear, day in and day out, and you'll get more life out of that equipment. What's more, time spent fondling all that gear is usually time spent fantasizing about snowboarding. The more time you spend mind-shredding and otherwise completely immersing yourself in the snowboarding lifestyle, the better snow-boarder you'll be. Snowboarding requires a certain level of obsession, and those obsessive tendencies are good for your gear.

TUNING EQUIPMENT

Although not essential to the pursuit of snowboarding, owning some tuning equipment is a good idea. Many companies sell kits with all the tools you need to keep your board tuned up, or you can find individual tools at local hardware stores and snow-board shops. Following is a list of the tools you should round up to keep your gear tuned and ready to rip.

File. A standard medium–coarse 8- to 10-inch file is a must for tuning and detuning your board. You can find one at any hardware store for a couple of bucks.

File brush. Your file won't work like it should if it's full of edge shards, so keep a file brush around to clean it up from time to time.

Compact edge tuner. A compact edge tuner can do the trick if you don't want to buy a file, plus it makes beveling your edges easier. Most models have guides that are adjustable from 85 degrees to 90 degrees in half-degree increments.

Plastic and metal scraper. You use these for scraping wax or P-tex.

Edge stone or diamond stone. For the finishing touches on any edge work swing by your local snowboard shop to buy a diamond stone. It's a good thing to carry whenever you're headed up to the mountain.

Gummy stone. Good for finishing off any tuning you do to your edges, a gummy stone will remove micro-burrs. Keep one in your pocket at all times, as you never know when you'll have a little snag to buff out. You'll have to go to a snowboard shop to buy a gummy stone.

Cleaning brush or scouring pads. These can be used to buff wax, or to simply clean up your workstation.

Base cleaner. Snow is filled with oil, sap, dirt, and all other forms of grime, so clean your base every time you wax it.

Vises/board stands. These allow you to mount your board vertically or horizontally. Most are made with anti-slip board grips to keep your board in place while you work on it. Also, look for stands that have easily adjustable C-clamps that can mount to any table.

Wax. All-temperature wax is your best bet, but if you know it's going to be really cold or warm, apply different types of wax accordingly.

Hot wax iron. A hot wax iron is different from a standard iron, being designed specifically for waxing snowboards.

P-tex. P-tex are polyethylene sticks used to fill in minor scratches in the base of your board. They're composed of the same material as your base, so you can melt them to repair gouges incurred by hitting rocks.

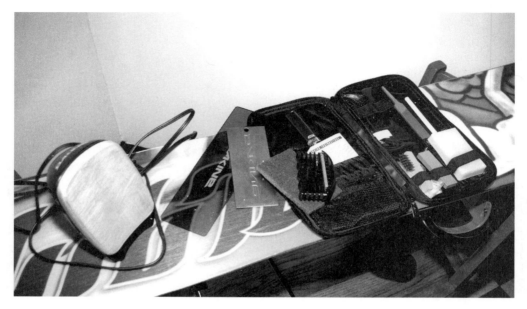

All the tuning equipment you'll need

SNOWBOARD PREP AND REPAIR

As your single most expensive piece of equipment, your snowboard should be your top priority when it comes to caring for your gear. Treating your snowboard right starts the minute you pull it out of the wrapper.

Snowboards come slightly *detuned—* that is, the edges are dulled at the contact points and around the tip and tail—but any board can use a little extra loving. A proper detune is the first order of business for any new board.

Sure, you can get by without it, but you may experience unexpected edge hooks in the worst possible places, like say, on icy cat tracks first thing in the morning or on rails on your last lap through the park. Sharp edges are prone to catch on the snow, so follow these steps to detune your new board and up your odds of staying all day long. You also want to occasionally detune your board throughout the season, as your board sustains abuse and the edges get kind of haggard.

HOW TO DETUNE

Before you get down to detuning, be sure to have a medium–coarse file, a gummy stone, and a diamond stone on hand.

The first step is to remove any major burrs on the edges. Give your board a first once-over with the file, buffing out any and all trouble spots on your edges. Survey the board for places where the edge has shavings sticking up or small nicks, and smooth them out with the file.

Next you want to detune the tip and tail of your snowboard. Find the widest part of your board at the nose and at the tail. Those are called the *contact points*. They are the sections of edge that make the most contact with the snow, and they're the first part of your edge to catch. Once you've found your contact points, start an inch back from them toward the center of your board, then use the file to round out the edge toward the nose or tail. You want to round the edges only slightly, because if you round off your edges too much you won't have any edge hold and that will cause you to slip out. Dulling these sections of the edge slightly helps the snow from unexpectedly grabbing your board, and hopefully keeps you from doing an unexpected face-plant.

After you've detuned the contact points, consider whether to do a light detune of both your toe edge and heel edge. If you live somewhere with really icy slopes or if you aspire to ride a lot of half-pipe or do a lot of carving, you probably don't need to detune these edges, because a sharper edge is an advantage in those icy conditions. But for most beginner and intermediate snowboarders, a full detune is a safe bet.

The best way to go about detuning the rest of your edges is to visually divide your edges into three sections. This will let you concentrate on smaller sections of your edge so you can keep your detune consistent. Detune each of the sections on each edge of your board individually, then move to the next.

When filing your edges, you want to place the file at about a 45-degree angle to the edge. Make one or two passes over each of the sections. The idea is to take just a little bit of the edge off.

Having detuned the entire length of your board, you want to remove all those edge shards with a cloth. This might seem like an unnecessary step, but know that all those micro-shards can end up in the base of your board and ultimately compromise its integrity. It's important to keep your base clean because that's what keeps your board sliding freely and fast.

Now go back and polish your edges with either a gummy stone or a diamond stone. Sure, that edge looks smooth, but in reality a lot of little micro-burrs probably need buffing out. It's also good to see if you have any rust on your edges; if so, use the diamond stone to buff out the rust.

"Sometimes people end up beveling their edge when they're detuning at the contact points, which doesn't really help. When you detune around your contact points, really round off the edges so they won't catch."

Cort Muller,
snowboard tuning technician

HOW TO WAX

A good wax is more important at certain times of the season, say, if it's bitter cold or crazy hot. Waxing your board can save you from bogging down in subzero powder or springtime slush. But waxing shouldn't be reserved for only the most extreme conditions. A regular wax helps keep the base of your shred sled from drying out and ultimately extends the life of your board.

To wax your snowboard, you need a hot wax iron, base cleaner, wax, scouring pads, and either a plastic or metal scraper.

The first step is to find a good place to work. Make sure you're set up in a well-ventilated area that you can get a little messy, since you're bound to drip and shave wax all over the place.

Before you wax, it's also a good idea to loosen the bolts on your board. If you run the iron over them, the bolts conduct heat and create small dimples in your base. To avoid this, you don't have to remove the bolts entirely. Just loosen them a little so you're waxing a nice, level base.

Your base will absorb wax better if it's good and clean, so scrape all the old wax off your board, then hit it with the base cleaner. One way is to simply use base cleaner and a rag. The more involved route is to run a hot iron over the base, apply a thin layer of wax, and instantly scrape it off. This "hot scrape" technique cleans your base by opening its pores, allowing any muck that's hiding in there to be pulled out. Keeping your base clean might not be much of an issue in the winter, but come spring

Be sure to drip wax evenly across the base of your board.

as all the fresh snow starts to melt and a winter's worth of debris makes its way to the surface, there can be lots of contaminants in the snow, so a good base cleaning is crucial.

Turn on your wax iron and set the temperature somewhere in the middle of the heat range. You don't want it too hot, because that will just burn up all your wax. If your wax iron starts smoking when you put the wax to it, then the iron's too hot.

Now you've got a decision to make: What

When you have enough wax on the base, use the iron to smooth out the drips and create a uniform coat of wax.

kind of wax will you use? You can never go wrong with a good all-temperature wax. Or you can choose a specific wax that suits the conditions (i.e., temperature and type of snow) you're riding in. If it's really cold out, choose a wax that's made for colder temperatures. Or, on the other hand, if it's warm, sunny, and slushy, you're going to need a wax designed for warmer weather. Snowboard waxes tend to be clearly labeled as to which temperature they're made for.

Melt the wax by holding it against the iron, and drip the wax all over the base of your board. Drip enough wax on the base to thinly cover the entire surface. Be extra liberal with wax along the edges, since that's the part of the base that sees the most friction and is usually the driest.

Now take the iron to the base and smooth the wax out into a nice, even coat. Keeping the iron moving constantly, do your best to spread the wax out evenly across the board. When you're happy with the coverage, set your board aside and allow it to dry for about 30 minutes, or until it goes down to room temperature. The base needs this time to absorb the wax, so don't rush it.

Once your board is cool and dry, get your scraper. Work with a sharp scraper so you aren't making the process harder for yourself. Scrape the surface of the base in long, smooth strokes. Short, choppy strokes can leave gouges in the wax and ultimately compromise your wax job. You should be left with a fine layer of wax covering the base. If you're worried about making a mess of your workspace, place a paper grocery bag at one end of your board and scrape the wax into it.

Now brush the base with the scouring pad to add structure to the wax. Structure helps water move away from your board. It might seem like you're buffing off all the wax you just applied to your base, but you're actually creating tiny channels that will steer water away from the base and cut down on suction.

"Put your hand on the top of your board to feel how hot the board is getting. It should never be more than warm to the touch. The only way to really damage your base is to leave the iron sitting in one place. Don't do that."

Scott Sparks, owner of Purl Wax

HOW TO BEVEL YOUR EDGES

When your board is shipped from the factory, its edges are 90-degree angles and almost razor-sharp. Brand-new edges can be a lot for any snowboarder to handle. They can catch you off-guard and send you to your face. To avoid this, file them to a slight bevel, moderating that 90-degree angle. Beveling your edges one or two degrees won't compromise their ability to carve, but it will keep them from catching when you least expect it. Anyone who's riding rails or boxes should bevel their edges in order to avoid edge hooks there, too.

To bevel your edges, you need a permanent marker and either a compact edge tuner or both a medium–coarse file and a file guide. If you don't have a file guide or a compact edge tuner, you can use tape; duct tape, electrical tape, or scotch tape will work.

Take the permanent marker and color in your board's entire edge. This will allow you to see exactly how much edge you're removing with every pass.

Using a compact edge tuner, first choose how much bevel you want to put on your edge. Most compact edge tuners offer either a 0- or a 2-degree bevel. To bevel with one of these tuners, simply position the tool so the file is in contact with the edge. Run the tuner up and down the edge of your board.

If you don't have a file guide, wrap one end of the file in tape so that it sits at an angle when placed on your base. Five or six wraps of tape should give you the bevel angle you're looking for.

Bevel the length of the effective edge, between the contact points. It's best to work small sections of the edge at a time, filing away at them until the pen marks are gone before moving onto the next section. Continue this process. Run the file back and forth along the edge until you can see that there's a slight angle to the edge. If you're not confident in your ability to bevel your edges, take your board to your snowboard shop.

HOW TO REPAIR YOUR BASE

Sooner or later, every snowboard takes a beating. Whether the culprit is an early season session or a mountain made of scree, your board is destined to get gouged. But with a metal scraper, some P-tex, and—ideally—a blowtorch, you can repair minor scratches at home.

The first step is to light your P-tex candle with a blowtorch, if you have one. While a lighter will work, typically its flame isn't hot enough, which can cause your P-tex to produce carbon deposits.

Once your candle is lit, you have to keep the flame blue. If you see yellow flame, you're holding your P-tex candle incorrectly. Once the candle is lit and a clear stream of molten P-tex is flowing from the end of it, move it down to the base of your snowboard.

A handheld blowtorch is the ideal tool for lighting P-tex, but a lighter will work, too.

Once your P-tex is lit it will begin to drip. Fill any gouges or scratches with this molten P-tex. Make sure you don't let any of the P-tex drip on your hand.

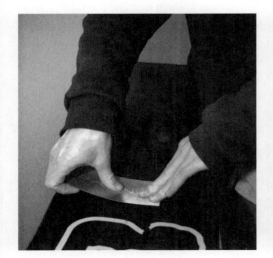

After you've filled the gouges use your metal scraper to press the P-tex down into the base of your board.

After the P-tex has cooled and hardened inside the gouge, scrape off the excess P-tex so you have a smooth base.

Keep the candle as close to the base as possible, with the tip of the clear P-tex stream just touching the board. If the P-tex is dripping onto the board in dots, you're holding the P-tex too high. Move the candle slowly around the base, filling all the gouges. When moving from one gouge to the next; try not to pick the candle up; just keep it right on the base and move to the next scratch. After you've filled the gouge with molten P-tex use your metal wax scraper to press the P-tex into the base.

After you've filled the gouge with molten P-tex, use your metal wax scraper to press the P-tex into the base.

After you're done filling scratches with the P-tex, let the P-tex cool to room temperature. Then use a metal scraper to scrape the excess P-tex off so you have a smooth base. Hold the scraper almost perpendicular to the base and scrape away from yourself. Don't be afraid to use some force to take the P-tex down. Scrape until you have a smooth base, and then apply a fresh coat of wax.

"Don't pick your candle up too high while you move it or you'll get a yellow flame and carbon deposits. As long as you keep that candle at the flow height and not the drip height, you will not get carbon deposits and your base will look great for resale and will ride incredible."

Bob Hawkins,
World Boards repair technician

Store your board so it's ready to ride opening day.

HOW TO STORE YOUR EQUIPMENT FOR THE OFF-SEASON

It's a sad day when you have to store your board for the summer. It'll be a while until you get to strap that thing onto your feet again, and that thought can inspire some real heartache. But don't stuff your board away without giving it the attention it needs and deserves. Take some time, tune it up, and tuck it into its place of rest so it's ready to go the next time the snow flies.

First, give the base a good once-over. Fill any gouges with P-tex, buff out any burrs or rust on the edges, and apply a liberal coat of wax. It's recommended that you leave the wax on pretty thick. The wax will protect the base as it gradually gets absorbed during the off-season.

Store your board in a cool, dry place. Avoid putting your board somewhere that gets a lot of direct sunlight. Somewhere dark and not too hot or cold is best. Never stack anything on top of your board, as the weight could flatten the board's camber and damage its flex and overall feel.

If your board came in a plastic sleeve and you held onto that synthetic sock of sorts, throw your board in there. Or, if you have a travel bag, use that for storage. Sleeving your board isn't essential, but keeping it out of sight might be the only thing that keeps your snow-starved mind from a breakdown during the summer months.

It's okay to leave the bindings on your board, but if you decide to remove them, mark where they were attached. That way,

the first snow day next year you won't have to struggle to remember what size stance you had. Outline your binders with a permanent marker, or put a few stickers down, or just jot down all the pertinent info (width, angles, etc.) somewhere you can track down later.

Your boots also deserve some attention. If your boots made it through the season and you hope to wear them again next winter, proper storage is essential. Lace them up so they hold their shape. Stuff them with newspaper to absorb some of the moisture that's sure to be trapped in those liners. And find a nice, dry place to store them, maybe next to your board. Damp, moldy basements are no place for your boots.

"I like to wax my board for the off-season. A thick coat of warm-weather wax is good so it won't crack during the summer and it will come off easier the next season."

Jussi Tarvainen

CHAPTER 7

Grabbing method like this is a lot easier if you're limber.

Fit to Ride

Make no mistake—snowboarding is a full-body workout. And thanks to its seasonal nature, every winter snowboarding serves to remind you of all the muscles you forgot you had. The off-season is long and, after seven idle months, many of us find our first day on snow really taxing on the body. But it doesn't have to be. While no activity perfectly mimics the use of muscles in snowboarding, many exercises and activities can make those first few runs (or first few days) a little less painful, especially when done right and in combination with each other.

Snowboarding works the lower body most intensely, but anyone who's spent the day riding knows that you can't get by with strong legs alone. To ride your best, you have to use your whole body. So, while you want to focus on working out your lower half, it's important to dedicate some time to strengthening your core and upper body as well.

To get ready for the winter and keep yourself in shape throughout the season, try to work out two to three times a week, allowing a day to rest in-between. Your goal is to build your endurance and strength, making sure that you work all of the major muscle groups you use while snowboarding.

Don't forget that preseason training can and should be fun. Choosing a variety of activities and exercises is the best way to make training something you enjoy. Try two to three bike rides a week, combined with some weight training to build muscles and endurance, and a couple of days of another board sport, like surfing or skating, to hone your balance.

The preseason is also the best time to indulge all those daydreams of waist-deep powder, bluebird days, and shredding with friends. Use the time you spend physically preparing for winter to also get your head in the right place. Consider it a holistic approach to the preseason. If you get your body ready to rip and also ride the mountain in your mind, you'll be able to snowboard strong right out of the gate.

BIKING

Riding a bike is a great way to cross-train for snowboarding in the off-season. A lot of the movements translate directly to snowboarding. Biking works the quads, calves, and core muscles, plus it's a great cardio workout. Any increase in your aerobic capacity will help when you head to the hills and are at altitude for the first time in a while. What's more, biking keeps your reflexes sharp by reminding you of the importance of things like picking a line, flowing downhill, always looking one turn ahead, and anticipating your next move.

STRETCHING

The main lower body muscles you use while riding are your quads, calves, hamstrings, groin, and gluteus. Spending time every day stretching all these muscles is guaranteed to improve your snowboarding. Flexibility plays a huge role in how you get down the mountain. Having limber limbs will sharpen your reaction time and allow you a little more room for error when you fall.

Remember, always stretch to the point of mild discomfort, not to the point of pain. And never bounce your stretches.

Make it a habit to do all these stretches before and after you ride as well.

LOWER BODY STRETCHES

Quad Stretch

1. In a standing position, lift your foot behind you and grab your ankle.
2. Point your knee to the ground and pull your foot up.
3. Stretch until the front of your leg (that is, the quad muscle) feels tight.
4. Hold for 20–30 seconds, then repeat with the other leg.

Standing Hamstring Stretch

1. Stand with your feet together or slightly apart.
2. Keeping your legs straight, reach down to the ground.
3. Breathe out as you reach down. Hold for 20–30 seconds.

Sitting Hamstring Stretch

1. Sit down on the floor with your legs fully extended and spread out like a V.
2. Reach both hands toward one of your feet.
3. Stretch until you feel the back of your upper leg tighten. Keep your knees flat on the floor. Breathe slowly and relax your back.
4. Hold for 20–30 seconds, then repeat with the other leg.

Gluteus/Hamstring Stretch

1. Lying on your back, bring one knee up to your chest.
2. Grab your knee with your hands and pull it toward you until you feel the stretch.

3. Hold for 20–30 seconds, then repeat with the other leg.

Lying Glute and Hip Stretch

1. Lie on your back with your legs extended and your back straight.
2. Bend your right knee and bring it toward your chest.
3. Grab your knee with your left hand and extend your right arm out to the side.
4. Keep your shoulder on the floor while using your left hand to pull your right knee across your body toward the floor on your left side.
5. Breathe and hold for 20–30 seconds. Then repeat with the other leg.

Butterfly Groin Stretch

1. Sit on the floor and put the soles of your feet together.
2. Grab your feet and gently bring them up toward your groin.
3. Now, holding your feet, lean forward.
4. Relax, breathe, and hold the stretch for 20–30 seconds.

UPPER BODY STRETCHES

In snowboarding, upper body flexibility is just as important as being limber in your lower body. Your upper body is the source of your sense of balance. Stretching gives you a wide range of motion in your upper body and in turn increases your ability to balance. Stretching your shoulders, neck, and back gives you better balance and quicker reaction time, as well as keeping you loose and prepared for the occasional (or all-too-frequent) fall.

Build up leg and core strength so you can power through powder all winter.

Shoulder Stretch

1. While standing, grab your left wrist with your right hand.
2. Pull your arm across your body, stretching your shoulder until it feels tight.
3. Hold for 20–30 seconds. Then repeat with the other arm.

Overhead Shoulder Stretch

1. Grab your right elbow with your left hand.
2. Pull your right elbow behind your head and stretch until it feels tight.
3. Hold for 20–30 seconds. Then repeat with the other arm.

Standing Chest Stretch

1. While standing or sitting upright, interlock your fingers behind your back and straighten your arms.
2. Lift your arms up behind you while keeping your back straight.
3. Breathe deeply and hold for 20–30 seconds.

EXERCISES

Snowboarding involves repetitive use (maybe even abuse) of the knees and hips, which means that the muscles surrounding those joints (the hamstrings, quads, glutes, and calves) need to be strong. It's equally important that these muscles have good endurance. You want to ride until last chair, right?

Try these exercises with light-to-medium resistance and a higher number of reps to help you develop strength and stamina in the muscles you use most.

STRENGTH EXERCISES FOR THE LOWER BODY

Squats

Squats are a great exercise for snowboarders because they work your quads, glutes, and hamstrings. To begin, stand with your feet spread as wide as they'd be if you were strapped into your board. Slowly lower your upper body, bending at your knees, until your thighs are parallel to the floor. Try varying your foot placement to give your glutes more of a workout.

Calf Raises

There's nothing like the burn from a long toeside traverse to make you wish you'd done some calf raises in the preseason. Since all you need is one stair, you've got no excuse for not doing them. Stand on the edge of the step with your heels hanging over. Lower your body and raise it up again. You can do either one leg at a time or both together. Put your hands on the wall to steady yourself, or try it without holding onto anything to work on your balance. Calf raises strengthen your calves as well as the muscles in your feet and around your ankles.

Lunges

Lunges are a great way to work your glutes and quads. Start in an upright position with your feet together. Step forward with one leg and lower your body until your knees bend to 90 degrees. Return to the upright position and switch legs. Try lunges wearing a backpack for more of a workout.

Hip Raises

Hip raises build strength in your hamstrings, glutes, and quads, which will ultimately make it easier to ride all day and feel balanced on your board. Start by lying on the floor with your arms at your sides, the soles of your feet on the floor, and your knees bent. Slowly lift your hips off the floor toward the ceiling and squeeze your glutes (the muscles in your butt). Return your hips to the floor and repeat.

STRENGTH EXERCISES FOR THE UPPER BODY

Your first day on the mountain usually makes it perfectly clear why you need to build upper body strength. You fall and have to get up a lot, and you use your shoulders, chest, biceps, and triceps to push yourself up. Build up those muscles in the preseason and you'll thank yourself later.

Upper body strength also helps keep you injury-free. Your upper body is bound to take a beating when you're learning to ride, and strong muscles protect your joints. When you fall, having good upper body strength can mean the difference between sore muscles and dislocated or broken bones.

These exercises will help keep you going all day while also hopefully allowing you to avert injury.

Push-ups

Push-ups are great for building strength in your shoulders, chest, triceps, and wrists—all parts of your body that you can expect to feel exhausted during your first few days on snow. Do push-ups just like your gym teacher taught you. Place your hands shoulder-width apart. Keeping your back straight, lower your chest to the ground and then push back up to the starting position. Repeat until you tire.

Dips

Like push-ups, dips build the muscles in your chest, shoulders, triceps, wrists, and forearms. To do a dip, start in a sitting position on the floor with your hands by your sides. Raise your butt off the floor. Lower your body by bending your shoulders and elbows. Then raise your body back to the starting position. Repeat until you tire.

EXERCISES FOR YOUR CORE

Core strength is also crucial to your success on the mountain. Your core connects your upper and lower body, and it's with these core muscles that you maintain your balance while riding. Your core muscles include your abdominals, obliques, lower back, and hips. A strong core helps you handle all types of terrain more easily, improves your balance, and hopefully keeps you injury-free.

Sit-ups

Your abdominal muscles get a lot of use in snowboarding, whether you're just cruising around the mountain or pushing yourself up

Strong legs make for solid slashes.

time and time again. During your first few days, you typically use your abs a lot more than you might imagine. So employ the age-old exercise of simply sitting up to build that core strength. Again, this is just like you learned in PE: Lie on your back and sit up. Then lie back down. Repeat until you tire.

Reverse Crunch

The reverse crunch is another great ab exercise for snowboarders. It offers all the same benefits as a sit-up. For this exercise, lie on the floor on your back, with your legs raised, your knees bent at a 90-degree angle, and your hands behind your head. Now bring your knees up toward your head and hold. Return your knees to the starting position. Repeat.

Genie Sit

Another relatively easy core-stregthening exercise is the genie sit, which helps build hamstring, glute, quad, outer thigh, and ab strength. To start, kneel on a mat or a rolled-up towel with your feet together and your knees slightly apart. Cross your arms over your chest and lean forward. Then lean back, making sure to keep your abs tight and your back straight. Pause and repeat until you tire.

Side Crunches

The side crunch is similar to the more widely known ab crunch, in which you lie on your back, raise your knees, cross your arms on your chest, and raise your chin toward your knees with your abs. It is used to strengthen the body's midsection, specifically the internal and external obliques. These are the muscles that help you rotate your body left and right. To do a side crunch, lie on your back with your bent knees turned to one side and resting on the floor. Put your hands behind your head and then bend forward like you would for normal crunches. Pull your knees over to the opposite side of your body and repeat until you tire.

CHAPTER 8

Cooke City, Montana, is a snowboarder's paradise. But, like all backcountry spots, it's rife with risks.

Introduction to
Backcountry Snowboarding

Time in the backcountry can be both awe-inspiring and terrifying. Being out in the mountains, sometimes miles away from civilization and all its amenities, is always a risky endeavor. Add the inherent dangers of snowboarding and you've got a lot of worst-case scenarios to consider. But prepare properly, educate yourself, and surround yourself with capable companions, and you'll discover the backcountry to be a place of unmatched beauty.

It can be a struggle to find this Shangri-la Getting into the backcountry requires a tremendous amount of preparation, a sizable investment in gear, a lot of learning, constant vigilance, and the ability to keep a cool head in even the most frightening situations. You or your friends could get buried in an avalanche, or a storm could move in and make it impossible to find your way out; then you're lost and might have to spend the night in the cold. A lot can go wrong,

but don't let that deter you. Odds are you're completely capable of handling anything the mountains might throw at you.

Snowboarding in the backcountry gets at that age-old idea of Man vs. Nature. It is a place to approach with respect. You can clear your head, find calm, spend time with friends, and push your abilities further. Is there any better place for a snowboarder?

ESSENTIAL GEAR

The first step to getting into the backcountry is making sure you have all the necessary equipment. The gear you pack can have a huge impact on the success of your time in the backcountry. Don't pack enough and you could find yourself hungry, thirsty, cold, and/or wet, and therefore in danger. Pack too much and you could break your back lugging all that extra gear around, not to mention how your ability to snowboard will be affected by that monkey on your back you call a pack.

Unlike resort riding, backcountry snowboarding requires you to bring more than just your board, boots, and bindings. Following is a list of the items you should *always* have with you. If a single one is missing, don't even think about going out into the backcountry.

Transceiver. Also called a beacon, the transceiver is the device used to locate people buried by avalanches. Transceivers aren't cheap. Expect to pay between $200 and $300 for one, but know that it'll be money well spent the minute you have to use it. Use the harness that comes with your transceiver and wear it next to your base layer of clothing.

Probe. Probes are long, collapsible poles that resemble tent poles. They're used to find avalanche victims buried under the snow.

Avalanche shovel. These specially designed shovels are smaller than most garden shovels and have removable handles. They're used for a variety of things in the backcountry, but most importantly when someone is buried by an avalanche you use this shovel to dig them out. A metal bladed shovel is best, as plastic shovels sometimes break.

Water. Water is a must. It might be cold, but that doesn't mean you won't get thirsty, so make sure you pack some water. The standard recommendation is one gallon of water per person per day. Hydration packs with built-in bladders are great, as are reusable water bottles. When it comes to packing water, bring as much as you can carry, because you'll always need it.

Snacks. You burn calories in the backcountry, so pack snacks like energy bars and dried fruit that give you energy without weighing down your pack. Chocolate or chocolate-covered espresso beans are also good for providing a boost of energy when you need it.

A standard backcountry pack and its contents: shovel, probe, transceiver, extra gloves and layers, first-aid kit, whistle, compass, lighter, snacks, water

Extra clothing. You never know when you'll need it, and it never hurts to have it. A lightweight shirt or fleece is a must-have. Extra glove liners are also good to carry.

First-aid kit. As essential as anything else on this list. Bandages, splints, antibiotic ointment, and gauze are important to have in case of minor injuries. Also be sure to have some over-the-counter painkillers. And make sure you include a whistle, too.

Knife. Any size will do, but the bigger the better. In an emergency you might have to use it to cut branches to build a shelter.

Matches or lighter. For building a fire.

Extra goggles. Goggles will fog. You might as well be able to see your way down the hill after that four-hour hike up.

Emergency blanket. A means of staying warm should you have to seek shelter for the night.

Cell phone. If you are headed somewhere there might be cell coverage, bring your phone. But don't expect that you'll have service, so by no means rely on a cell phone as your safety net.

Map. Not only will you need a map of the backcountry you're riding, but you'll also have to know how to read that map.

Compass. A compass is one of the oldest tools available. Buy one and learn how to use it before you venture out.

Flashlight. You never know when you'll get caught out after dark. A flashlight can be a lifesaver if you find yourself stranded.

The backcountry is a wild place in the most literal sense of the word. No ski patrollers are nearby to rescue you should the worst happen. And the worst can and does happen. In the backcountry, there are those who have dealt with bad situations and those who will … which is to say, it's just a matter of time. Weather can roll in, daylight can fade, you can get lost, and you could have to spend the night out.

In case you have to hunker down until daylight, having the following extra items in your pack could save your life, but they are also good to have with you anytime. Carrying these can make those inevitable bad situations at least bearable.

Extra gloves. Hands sweat, sweat cools, hands get cold and go numb.

Extra hat. Head sweats, sweat cools, head gets cold, and then you're done for.

Thicker extra layers. Pick something that isn't too heavy but will provide warmth when you need it.

A candle. If you have to spend the night in a snow cave, a candle can heat the cave until the morning.

Satellite phone. A satellite phone is expensive, but if you spend a lot of time in the backcountry, it's a good investment. If you end up having to use one, it will be worth whatever it cost.

Two-way radios. Handheld two-way radios are the best way to communicate with friends in your group or, if need be, other groups that might be in the area.

To carry your backcountry gear, you need a pack. Your backcountry pack should be smaller than, say, your standard book bag. A lot of companies make packs specifically designed for the backcountry snowboarder.

These packs are built to fit only what you need and nothing more. If you're packing for a day in the backcountry and you find yourself running out of room, maybe it's time to take a look at what you're packing.

When buying a pack, make sure you find one that fits well, as you don't want to end up with a pack that's awkward to ride in. Try loading it up at the shop to see how it will ride when you're geared up and out in the elements.

BETTER SAFETY THROUGH TECHNOLOGY

Knowledge of the backcountry is essential in order to stay safe out there, but thanks to advancements in technology, backcountry enthusiasts can now buy equipment that reduces some of the risks they face when out-of-bounds. Remember that equipment is no substitute for experience, and none of this gear guarantees that you will make it back from the backcountry. Consider this equipment as complementary to know-how. Educate yourself first, then buy the gear you think you'll need.

THE AVALUNG

These devices are quickly becoming must-have equipment among snowboarders who frequent the backcountry. Developed by Black Diamond, the AvaLung essentially lets you breathe when buried under snow. It works as an artificial air pocket, allowing you to pull oxygen from the snow surrounding you. The AvaLung is just a tube with a mouthpiece and an apparatus that allows you to inhale oxygen trapped in the snow. When you exhale through the same mouthpiece, your breath is directed to a different part of the snowpack so as to avoid CO_2 poisoning, which can ultimately kill you. Two models of the AvaLung are on the market right now. One is a stand-alone item and the other is integrated into backpacks. Although it's a new technology, it's already proving it works, and it's sure to be used by more and more snowboarders every year.

> "I have three friends who probably would've died this winter from falling in tree wells and getting buried by snow if it wasn't for the Avalung. That's all the proof I need."
>
> *Lucas Debari*

RECCO

The Recco system sends out a signal that bounces off a small reflector sewn into all kinds of snow garb; a device then detects the reflected signal, allowing rescuers to locate whoever is wearing the gear. Recco was first developed in 1973 in Sweden by Manus Granhed after he witnessed an avalanche rip down his home mountain and bury a bunch of local skiers. He helped with the rescue attempts and quickly realized there had to be a better way to locate avalanche victims.

Today more than 400 rescue organizations and 350 ski resorts use the Recco system. Quiksilver, Vans, Volcom, Sessions, and Billabong are just a few of the outfitters

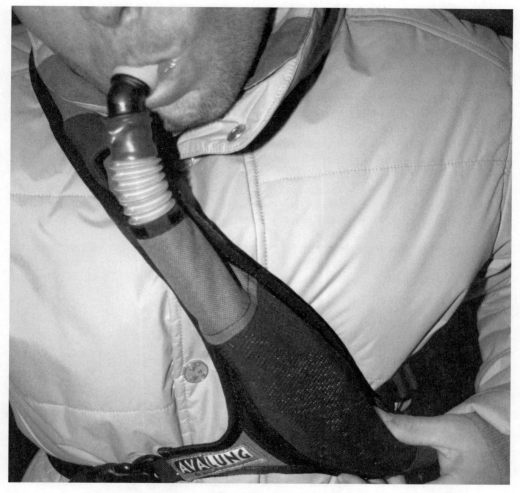

The AvaLung allows you to breath when buried by extracting oxygen in the snow through this mouthpiece.

including Recco in their lines. So now your outerwear can be simultaneously stylish and equipped to save your ass. Consider this statistic: Last season 50 percent of the avalanche victims who didn't survive weren't wearing any kind of beacon or Recco-equipped outerwear. Food for thought for next time you're buying outerwear.

HOW TO PREPARE FOR THE BACKCOUNTRY

Hope for the best, but plan for the worst. Cliché maybe, but sound advice nonetheless for anyone headed into the backcountry. Simple truth: Backcountry snowboarding is no lap in the park.

While many of the backcountry images that surface paint a sublime picture of backcountry snowboarding, know that these photos are the result of a lot of preparation.

You could spend your life learning about the backcountry and still not be fully prepared for everything Mother Nature might throw at you. It's a wild world out-of-bounds, and being prepared for a backcountry outing can mean the difference between life and death. However, make the right preparations and your backcountry experience will be one defined by triumph not tragedy.

The first thing anyone who's headed into the backcountry should do is take an avalanche awareness class. Typically these classes spend a day or two in the classroom learning about snowpack, avalanche scenarios, how to test conditions in the field, how to use your transceiver,

Staying close to your buddies is crucial in the backcountry. If one stops to take a break, others should do the same.

and how to rescue your friends should they get caught in an avalanche. Then the class heads outdoors into the snow to show you how to actually use all the skills you've covered. Expect to pay a couple hundred dollars for one of these classes, which is a small price in exchange for a solid understanding of the conditions that contribute to avalanches and how to react when the worst happens.

As important as it is for you to attend one of these classes, it's even more important that the people accompanying you into the backcountry enroll as well. It's crucial that you be able to trust the people you're shredding with. Get your friends to take the class with you, so you can surround yourself with snowboarders who know what they're doing in the backcountry.

Go into the backcountry with a crew that you get along with. Days in the backcountry can be long and grueling. Pick your posse accordingly. It's also best to go out with riding partners who are at the same skill level as you and are looking to hit the same type of terrain.

"Taking an avalanche safety class before you go into the backcountry is one of the best things you can do. There is so much to learn about the way snow falls, accumulates, settles, is blown around, freezes or heats up, and on and on. Ignorance can cost you your life. Make sure your friends are educated, too. If you get in a bad situation, they are the ones who will be helping you out."

Amber Stackhouse

MONITORING WEATHER CONDITIONS

Knowing what the weather conditions are going to be (or might be) is the next step. Check the local weather forecast and avalanche report before you even consider heading out. Sites like www.noaa.gov, www.avalanche.org, and www.weather.gov can give you an idea about what's going on out there.

Cross-reference a couple of websites to see if the forecasts are consistent. If it looks like the conditions will be safe, head for the hills, but remember, just because the forecasters give you a green light doesn't mean you can stop surveying the situation.

Don't forget to employ your own powers of observation. As soon as you leave your house, look outside. Notice what the weather did in town, and try to figure out how that translates to the surrounding mountains.

On your way to the hill, keep your eyes open. Notice how the slopes are loaded. What kind of snow fell? Is it heavy or light? Did the wind blow last night? Do certain slopes look scoured or loaded? Pay attention to your surroundings and you'll see there are clues everywhere.

"Listening to your gut instinct is everything in the mountains. The important thing is to leave all outside pressures in the parking lot so you are open to the signals the mountains are sending you. Like John Muir said, 'Mountains speak, wise men listen.'"

Jeremy Jones

When you are in the backcountry, pay attention to which way the wind is blowing, so you can determine which aspects of the mountains are safest to shred.

UNDERSTANDING AVALANCHES

On average, 100 people die in avalanches in North America and Europe every year.

By choosing to snowboard in the backcountry, you're choosing to put yourself in harm's way. Acknowledge that fact, educate yourself about the dangers, keep your skills sharp and your senses alert, and odds are you won't become a statistic.

Most avalanches occur on slopes between 30 and 45 degrees, but don't discount pitches that are less steep. A wetter snow pack might be prone to sliding on a mellower grade. If you're not sure how steep the slope is, learn to use an inclinometer or slope meter and

WEATHER FORECAST SOURCES

After more than twenty years of forecasting mountain weather and avalanche conditions, I am still learning. In fact, learning about weather, snow, and avalanches is a journey rather than an event. We know mountains act as weather-makers and weather-breakers, and a key lesson learned—and it has motivated me to keep studying—is that no matter how much better forecasting has gotten over the years (and it has gotten a whole lot better), a forecast that is completely right for an entire mountain range can be completely wrong on one particular mountain. To reduce these sorts of surprises, it's important that you become your own forecaster by learning to read clouds, winds, temperatures, and changes in atmospheric pressure.

When checking weather, my first stop is the Colorado Avalanche Information Center's website (http://avalanche.state.co.us) because they prepare a solid mountain weather forecast. A number of the U.S. avalanche centers also prepare local mountain weather forecasts, too. If the weather is expected to make a significant change, I follow up with visits to the National Weather Service's site (www.weather.gov) and specifically to the pages of the local forecast offices. I read a forecast product called the "Area Forecast Discussion." This provides a short summary of the weather-making patterns and the metrological reasoning that went into preparing local forecasts. Because I've forecast weather and avalanches for over twenty years, I am a weather nerd and snow junkie. To get the best fix of the raw weather stuff, I also spend time on www.weather.unisys.com. This site offers all the weather maps, charts, satellite and radar images, and data I need to develop my own mountain weather forecasts. What's cool about the Unisys site is you can see weather maps for the rest of the world—and the best part about all these sites is that the information is free!

Dale Atkins, avalanche expert

keep it with you at all times.

Another key factor to consider is the aspect of the slope. Aspect refers to the direction the slope faces—north, south, east, west, or any of the directions in-between. The aspect of the mountainside determines how much sun or shade the snow gets, which affects the stability of the snowpack.

During winter, most avalanches run on the north, east, and northeast slopes. Come spring, when the mountains see more sun and experience a lot of freezing and thawing, you see a lot of wet slide avalanches on the south-facing slopes.

Avalanches can happen anytime, but statistically most happen during or right after

Always hike with friends you trust.

a snowstorm. Keep this in mind when planning an outing. If it just dumped or is still dumping, be extra wary of the snowpack.

Always check the avalanche danger level before you head into the backcountry. Your local avalanche center can give you a good idea about the snow's stability. And remember, this is a source of information about the dangers you might be facing, but don't let it be your only source.

Once you get into the backcountry, start making your own observations to figure out the amount of avalanche danger. You can perform a number of tests to see just how stable the snow is, and the more tests you try the better.

One of the simplest tests is done with a trekking pole or your probe. Poke it into the snow, seeing if you can detect any distinct layers. Ask yourself: How deep is the

Always check the local avalanche forecast before you head into the backcountry.

snowpack? Do I feel any distinct layers that might not be bonded together? Notice any cracks in the top layers of snow.

Keep an ear out for the distinct "Whumph" sound snow makes when it settles. You'll know it when you hear it. If you do hear it, odds are the snow is unstable and you should head for the car.

To get an even more accurate evaluation of the snowpack, dig a pit in the snow. This allows you to closely observe any weak layers in the snow. Your pit should be at least 3 feet deep and on a slope that's similar to the one you plan to shred. Pay close attention to any inconsistency in the snowpack.

There are a few different types of tests you can use, but the shear test should give you a good enough sense of the snow's

ANATOMY OF AN AVALANCHE

Contrary to popular belief, avalanches involving people don't happen randomly. In 92 percent of avalanche accidents, the victim or someone in their party triggers the slide. Since we place ourselves in harm's way for the sake of recreation, it's a good idea to understand what's happening with the snow. Only then can we play safely in avalanche terrain.

Dry slab avalanches account for almost all avalanche deaths. A slab is a cohesive mass of snow that slides on an underlying, weaker layer. Dry slab avalanches are dangerous because they have a tendency to fracture once we're already on the slope. Their release can come as a deadly surprise.

Most avalanche fatalities happen on small slopes less than 300 vertical feet in size. Yet even something small can have deadly consequences. Avalanches accelerate quickly and can reach speeds over 80 mph, which doesn't leave you much time to react. Additionally, the weak layer under the slab can propagate at over 200 mph, appearing to fracture the slab all at once. The slope shatters like a pane of glass. Additionally, you've got chunks of slab tumbling with you. Imagine a few trees and rocks on the slope, and you can see why getting caught can be serious business.

In order for us to produce an avalanche, we need four basic ingredients. If any of these is missing, an avalanche isn't possible. The first ingredient is avalanche terrain: an open slope more than 30 degrees steep. Unfortunately, this is also the prime angle for snowboarding. For reference, a black diamond ski run is usually between 35 and 40 degrees. The second ingredient is a slab of snow, a relatively dense and cohesive layer. The third ingredient is a weak layer underlying the slab. When this weak layer fails, the slab becomes unsupported, causing it to fracture and tumble down. And, lastly, we need a trigger. A trigger is something that tips the scales by adding more stress to the snowpack, causing an avalanche. Natural triggers include the weight of more snow or the impact from a cornice falling. However, we're most worried about human triggers. In 92 out of every 100 avalanche accidents, we're the ones releasing the avalanches that kill us.

There are many times during the winter when dry slab avalanches can be on the brink of fracturing. Like the straw that breaks the camel's back, the weight of a person can sometimes initiate a fracture. This is because sudden stress, like the weight of a snowboarder, can cause weak layers to fail. If the weak layer is widespread, the slab will be on the verge of avalanching.

Most of us choose to play in avalanche terrain, so right off the bat we've got two of the four ingredients: a steep slope and us, a trigger. Let's take a look at the other two ingredients.

Every time it snows, a new layer is added to the snowpack. Warm weather can create denser layers; the sun can form ice crusts; cold, clear nights can form surface hoar. Some of these layers are stronger or weaker than others, and it's the relationship between them that determines the avalanche danger. When a relatively stronger, denser layer overlies a weaker one, we have the remaining two ingredients. Some slabs, like those densely packed by the wind, resemble cement blocks. Others are far softer. For an avalanche, we need a slab of snow that's stronger than the layer of snow underneath. Sometimes even powder can fracture and act as a slab if it's sitting on something even weaker.

Weak layers are a major piece in the avalanche puzzle, yet they can be tricky to identify. We've repeatedly seen similar types of weak layers fail and cause avalanches. Surface hoar is a top performer. This frozen dew forms feathery crystals that become persistent weak layers once they're buried. The same goes for faceted, angular crystals that look and feel like sugar. These are formed by strong temperature gradients in the snowpack and are poorly bonded. A good test is to try to make a snowball out of a handful of them. It doesn't work.

These avalanche basics are the first step in trying to answer the question "Can the slope slide?" Does it have the four ingredients? Perhaps it already has three of them, but is missing the fourth: you. Whether a slope avalanches is all about the timing or convergence of these ingredients.

Doug Chabot, director,
Gallatin National Forest Avalanche Center

stability. Once you've dug your pit, isolate a column of snow. Stick your shovel behind the column, on the uphill side of it, and pull the shovel handle toward you. If very little pressure brings the column crashing down, you're dealing with a weak snowpack and should probably call it a day. If it takes a good pull to free the column, then you're working with a stable snowpack and you should be good to go. That doesn't mean you can throw caution to the wind. Back-country snowboarding requires constant attention to the conditions, as they can change in an instant.

You can never be too cautious in the backcountry. It can take a lifetime to learn all the nuances of mountain weather, snowpack, and the conditions you might encounter. But if you start educating yourself now and keep learning more every season, you'll be able to recognize and avoid the dangers that exist in the backcountry.

HELPING OTHERS IN THE BACKCOUNTRY

Even with proper planning and knowledge of the current snowpack, you're never completely safe when venturing into the backcountry. At some point in your snowboarding career, things will go wrong. It's impossible to anticipate everything that can go wrong, but if you take the time to take precautions, educate yourself, and keep a cool head, you'll be in the best position to manage whatever situation you come across.

Make sure you know first aid and CPR. Take a class, or classes, and have your buddies do the same. You'll learn how to deal with minor injuries, but more importantly, these classes will teach you to remain level-headed when you most need to. Increased confidence is incredibly valuable when the worst happens. Often the key to dealing with any backcountry injury is to avoid making the victim worse than they already are.

When it comes to performing first aid, know that you might have to improvise, especially in a wilderness situation. If you're really getting out there, you owe it to yourself and to your crew to take a wilderness first-aid class or commit to a lengthier wilderness first-responder course. Visit the National Outdoor Leadership School (NOLS) website at www.nols.edu for more info.

If you find yourself with a life-threatening emergency, call for help immediately. Use your cell phone if you have service, or a satellite phone if you have one, and communicate your GPS coordinates so that help can reach you quickly. If you're starting to risk your life in the backcountry, a satellite phone is worth the investment. If you have neither a cell phone nor a satellite phone, send someone in your group for help. The person with the most medical training should stay with the injured person, and the fastest person should go for help.

"Do whatever it takes to get your friend to safety. Don't worry about the bill. If someone is really hurt and you can call with a cell phone and get a $3,000 heli-lift out, do it."

Dave Downing

MEANS OF ACCESS: AN INTRODUCTION TO THE BEST WAYS TO GET INTO THE BACKCOUNTRY

You've taken the classes, bought the equipment—and learned to use it—,checked the forecasts, and assembled your posse; now how do you reach that promised land? Depending on your budget and your desires, you've got some options.

ACCESS GATES

Backcountry access gates are like warp zones. Step through that portal and you're instantly transported to a wonderfully serene world with untracked powder in every direction and only a few other snowboarders

AMBER STACKHOUSE DISCUSSES GETTING CAUGHT IN AN AVALANCHE

Liam: Have you ever been caught in an avalanche?

Amber: Yes, but in the grand scheme of slides, it was really very minor.

Liam: What happened?

Amber: I was in a backcountry area outside of Salt Lake City, on a sunny day in April when the avalanche warning was just at "moderate." About a foot of fresh snow had fallen the night before, and temperatures were rising rapidly. Rapid condition changes create a breeding ground for slides, so I should have been more cautious. Instead, with the filmer and photographer a couple hundred yards away on the other side of the gulch, I decided to cut a wide turn across a steep northern face for a mellow powder spray shot.

As soon as I started my line across the slope, the snow released. I was traveling in front of it and heard the photographer and filmer yell. That was the only way I knew anything had happened. In haste, I thought I would just point it down the short slope and use my momentum to ride up the other side of the gully. Due to the warm, sticky snow, I barely made it up the other side of the gully at all. I lunged as far up it as I could get and waited for the sliding snow to hit me, still unaware of how much snow had actually slid. The snow piled up around me. I was lucky that the hill wasn't longer or I would have been in much more serious trouble. As it was, the 1-foot-deep, 50-foot-across wind slab that I triggered buried me to my thighs with cement-like chunks of snow. In retrospect, my escape plan was flawed. I should have angled off the side and gotten out of the way, rather than head right for the same place the snow was headed. Again, I was lucky it was not a longer slope or deeper snow.

Liam: What was going through your mind while you were caught?

Amber: I was not that concerned, because I was in front of the slab and I could not actually see the slide. I figured it was just a really tiny sluff slide. After it was over and I saw the debris track, I got more freaked out. I felt that my "escape" strategy of gaining speed to climb the opposing gully wall was stupid and could have gotten me into serious trouble if the slope had been a bit longer or if the new layer of snow a bit deeper. It freaked me out to know that in a real situation my instincts were wrong.

Liam: What should everyone know about getting caught in an avalanche?

Amber: The most important thing is to be prepared and do your best to avoid it in the first place. Wear a beacon; ride with a friend who also has a beacon, shovels, and probes; train yourself on proper beacon use; and pay attention to the current snow and weather conditions.

Liam: What should people do if they get caught?

Amber: If it is a slab slide and you can get above the fracture line, do it fast. If that doesn't work and you are sliding with it, try to hold your speed and outrun it or angle out of it and to the side. If that still doesn't work, try to grab onto a tree before the slide picks up too much speed. If there are no trees, start swimming. Our bodies are way heavier than snow, so you need to fight gravity and swim to stay afloat. Try to clear an air space around your mouth, and stick an arm up, if you can figure out which way that is. The air will help keep you alive longer, and the hand will help rescuers locate you. Do this all before the slide stops, because even in a small one like mine, the snow turns to concrete as soon as it settles to a stop.

Liam: Single best piece of advice you've received concerning avalanches?

Amber: Educate yourself.

seeking to destroy it all. Since these gates can be accessed from resorts, they offer snowboarders who are new to the backcountry a convenient means to an ultimately radical end. But even though these gates are easy to get to, don't forget that the terrain on the other side is deserving of your respect.

Most of the 130 U.S. resorts that operate on Forest Service land offer backcountry access gates. Some are always open; others are closed at times due to avalanche danger. If you're uncertain which is the case for the gates at the resort you're riding, check with the ski patrol before you venture out.

Backcountry is backcountry, and it's inherently dangerous—it's as simple as that. So safety should be of the upmost concern when you're using a backcountry gate. Always carry your backcountry pack, and don't even think about setting foot through one of these gates without a buddy—or better yet, buddies—who

can save you should things go bad.

Remember that once you leave the resort, there won't be any signs out there. Be sure you know your route back. Also, always consider how much daylight you have left before you begin your adventure, so you don't end up having to spend a night in the woods.

A few of the resorts with backcountry gates offer educational courses to teach fledgling backcountry enthusiasts about all the dangers that exist beyond the boundaries. Check to see if your local resort offers a class. If it does, enroll. It could save your life or the lives of your friends.

Always keep in mind that just because the gate is open doesn't mean the snow is stable. Check your local avalanche center for current conditions and any avalanche advisories. Evaluate the snow yourself once you're on the hill. And when in doubt, don't go out.

CAT BOARDING

Cat boarding could very well be the best introduction to the backcountry. You're shuttled to and from all the best stashes on the snowcat. You get to indulge in hot drinks on the ride up, recount the run with your buddies on the way back, or just sit back and enjoy the view. You've also got a qualified staff of guides keeping an eye out and otherwise ensuring that you're staying safe. You'll never have to dig the snowcat out (like you inevitably would with a snowmobile), and you'll never be grounded because of bad weather (as is often the case when relying on helicopters).

What more could you want?

Most cat operations are required to have licensed guides who are trained in avalanche science and wilderness first aid. And these guides are paid to know the terrain like the back of their mittens, so you know you'll be taken to the best and safest spots on the mountain.

You should be at least an advanced-intermediate shredder to even think about signing up for a day of cat boarding. You've got to be able to handle yourself and your board in all kinds of terrain before you even consider climbing into a cat.

Because there's sure to be a risk of avalanches where you're shredding, most cat-boarding outfits require that you know how to use a transceiver, and if you don't, they'll show you how prior to heading for the hills. It's best to come prepared with your own backcountry pack, but if you're without your gear, the operator might be able to provide you with some.

You can expect to make seven to ten runs and log anywhere from 8000 to 18,000 vertical feet of freshies on an average day of cat boarding. Prices vary depending on what kind of experience you're looking for, but expect to pay no less than $300 a day. Most cat companies will have discounted rates at the beginning or end of the season. Or see if the operation offers group discounts and round up a bunch of your buddies.

Ski resorts across the country—from Keystone in Colorado to Whitefish Mountain Resort in Montana—offer cat-boarding daytrips for those looking to complement a day of resort riding. For the full lodge experience, places like Baldface Lodge in British Columbia or Peak Adventures in Idaho offer all the shredding and après amenities you could ever need.

SNOWMOBILES

Snowmobiles inspire a lot of love/hate feelings. They allow you to access all kinds of terrain you might otherwise have never known existed, but they also require constant maintenance and are notorious for breaking down in all the wrong places. But if it's remote wilderness you're seeking out and you've got the time, money, and patience to dedicate to one, a snowmachine is the ultimate snowboarding accessory.

Before you go and rent or buy a snowmobile (aka "sled"), here's one statistic to consider: Snowmobilers account for 33 percent of the backcountry enthusiasts killed by avalanches. You definitely need to know something about the risk

Snowmobiles tip over. Remember to kill the engine as soon as you roll your sled, so you don't flood the engine. Then, find a friend to help you out.

of avalanches before you head out on your snowmobile. Again, take the time to really educate yourself about all the dangers of the backcountry. It's equally important to learn a thing or two about how to operate a snowmobile.

When you're just getting into snowmobiling, it's best to head into the backcountry with someone who has experience on a sled. Also, do some research on the terrain you'll be in. As with any other backcountry outing, always check the weather and avalanche forecasts before you leave.

You need to carry safety equipment on your snowmobile in case (or rather, when) something goes wrong. You never want to be without your backcountry pack, a tool kit, a compass, flares, and an extra ignition key. A GPS unit isn't a bad idea either. A lot of today's pro snowboarders also carry satellite phones, as most snowmobile into areas where cell phones don't get service.

Snowmobiles break down, so be prepared to do some on-hill repairs. Have a tool kit that includes all of the following at a minimum:

- Screwdrivers—Phillips and flathead
- Pliers

- Spare spark plugs and a spark-plug wrench
- Adjustable crescent wrench
- Electrical tape
- Spare belts
- Tow strap

"Use your body weight to turn and keep the sled going in the direction you want it to go. Gas is usually your friend and can get you out of bad situations, so don't be afraid of the throttle. Always look ahead. If for some reason you can't make it up a hill, you have to figure out a way down, so always be looking around, scanning for escape routes. And most importantly, never stop your sled on an uphill slope unless you want it to get stuck."

Wille Yli-Luoma

HELICOPTER SNOWBOARDING

Sure, heli-boarding might seem like a fanciful pipe dream for most of us, but you never know where snowboarding will take you. Maybe the day will come when you find yourself on a heli trip. It never hurts to hope, right?

Beginners shouldn't even think about helicopter snowboarding, but the advanced-intermediate snowboarder could probably handle some of the snowboarding that select heli operations offer. As a rule of thumb, if you can't make it down every run at your local hill, you've got no business climbing into a helicopter. Learn to shred hard, start saving your money, and then when you're good and ready (both physically and financially), look into a heli trip.

Not all helicopter operations are created equal. Same goes for the mountains you'll be flying into and down. Decide what kind of terrain you want to ride and do some research. Find an outfit that suits your ability, tastes, and budget. Check out www.helicopterskiing.org for more information about all kinds of heli outfits.

Know what kind of riding you're going to do and pack accordingly. A lot of lodges offer loaner backcountry packs, but honestly if you're considering heli-snowboarding, this should be something you already own.

Know your equipment. Make sure everything is in working order. Bring enough to get by on during your trip, but don't bring too much, as most outfits will limit the number of bags you can bring. Think like a minimalist.

You can buy travel insurance that'll reimburse you should something happen and you have to call the whole thing off. Look into it; it could save you a couple G's.

A heli-snowboarding trip can be the experience of a lifetime, if you score. But sometimes the universe conspires against us. Weather moves in, snow gets unstable, someone gets hurt. Simply put: Shit can happen. Be patient if things don't go as you'd hoped. Make the most of down days if they should arise. Appreciate your surroundings—even if you're stuck in a lodge, at least it's a lodge in the middle of nowhere. If you've made it that far, you're a lot better off than most people. Don't forget that.

Glossary

air Any time you leave the ground on your snowboard.

air-to-fakies A half-pipe trick that involves no rotation; you air out of the pipe and land.

airing out Any time you catch air.

Andrecht A handplant in which you plant your trailing hand and grab your board with your leading hand.

ankle strap The strap on your binding that wraps around your ankle.

approach zone The zone from which you approach a feature.

backside 180 Half of a full rotation spun backside; you land switch or fakie.

backside 360 (backside three, back three) A full rotation spun backside; you land regular, or facing the same direction you were when you left the lip.

backside 540 One and a half rotations spun backside; you land switch, or facing the opposite direction you were when you left the lip.

backside air An air done in the half-pipe in which you pop off your heel edge.

backside spin A spin in which regular riders turn clockwise in the air; goofy footers turn counterclockwise when doing a backside spin.

base plate The part of your binding that connects to the snowboard.

beacon A device that transmits a frequency that can be detected, or received, by other beacons; used to locate and rescue avalanche victims. Also called *transceiver*.

binding (binder) The device that attaches your boot to a snowboard.

blower Light, fluffy powder snow.

board edge The metal edge of your snowboard.

boardslide A railslide in which the board slides perpendicular to the rail or box.

boost To catch a lot of air.

C-shaped rail A rail curved like the letter C.

camber The arch of a snowboard. A board's

camber is most visible when the board is set on a flat surface.

cap strap A binding toe-strap that wraps around the entire toe box of your boot.

cat boarding Using a snow cat to access backcountry terrain.

cat tracks The wide, flat trails made by snowcats at resorts.

contact points The sections of a snowboard's edge just below the nose and tail.

coping The lip of a half-pipe; a slang term borrowed from skateboarding.

corked out A spin or trick that's done off-axis or inverted.

counter-rotate To rotate your upper body in the opposite direction you're going to spin, just prior to takeoff.

deck The flat section of a jump between the lip and the landing. Also refers to the flat section that borders a half-pipe.

detune To file down the edges of your snowboard so they aren't so sharp.

dialed in Having a good understanding, either of how your gear should fit or how to do a trick.

down rail A rail that is angled downhill.

down-flat-down rail A kinked rail that is angled downhill, then flat, and then downhill again.

drop-in To turn downhill to approach a feature.

edge hold The way your snowboard edges hold against the snow; sharp edges hold or grip the snow better than dull edges.

edge hook Board edges hooking or catching against the snow; not a good thing.

effective edge The length of a snowboard's edge that actually comes in contact with the snow.

fakie Riding backward, so what's regularly your trailing foot is treated as your leading foot. Also called *switch*.

fall line The path that an object would naturally take down a slope. For a snowboarder the fall line is the path your board wants to slide down.

50-50 A rail slide in which your board is pointed in the same direction as the rail you're sliding and your edges are parallel to that rail.

flat-based Riding your board with the entire base in contact with the snow (i.e., not using your edges).

flat-bottom The middle or bottom of the half-pipe; the space between the transitions.

flat-down rail A rail that is flat to begin with, then angles downhill.

flat rail A rail that doesn't have any uphill or downhill angle

flow To ride effortlessly and stylishly.

freestyle terrain Any terrain that has jumps, rails, boxes, jibs, half-pipes, or other man-made features designed for freestyle snowboarding.

freshies Fresh snow; powder; new snow.

frontside 180 Half a rotation spun frontside; you land riding away fakie, or switch.

frontside 360 (frontside three) A full rotation spun frontside; you land riding away regular, or in the direction you were facing when you left the lip.

frontside 540 (frontside five) One full rotation and another half rotation spun frontside; you land riding away fakie or switch, facing the opposite direction you were when you left the lip.

frontside air Any jump or ollie on your frontside wall in the half-pipe.

frontside boardslide A boardslide in which your board is perpendicular to the rail but your heel edge is your leading edge.

frontside spin A spin in which your toe edge is the leading edge in the direction you're spinning; you bring your trailing leg forward or downhill.

fun box A box made out of metal and plastic that is meant to be slid on a snowboard.

goofy Riding with your right foot as your leading foot.

grab Technique in which you grab your board in the air and hold on for a moment.

groomers Ski runs at a resort that are groomed by snowcats.

half-pipe A large, man-made ditch that resembles half of a pipe.

handplant A maneuver in which you put your hand down on the snow and balance on it for a moment. Also called *invert*.

hard pack Snow that's packed down hard.

heelside The edge of the snowboard that is underneath or behind a rider's heels. Also used to mean turns made on the heelside edge. Also *heel edge*.

highback The piece of a binding that sits flush against your calf, providing support and responsiveness.

hiking Putting one foot in front of the other to get yourself up the mountain with your snowboard.

hip A jump in which you land at a perpendicular angle to the takeoff.

hit a jump To go off a jump.

huck To jump recklessly or out of control.

in-run The section just uphill of the jump or feature; also known as the approach zone.

invert See handplant.

inverted To flip or turn upside-down during a trick.

jib Snowboarding on any object that isn't necessarily meant to be ridden.

knuckle The section of a jump between the deck and the landing, basically the edge of the landing; not a good place to land.

landing zone The section of a jump that's angled downhill; the best place to land.

lapping Repeating the same run several times.

last chair The last chairlift ride of the day.

leading The downhill edge, hand, arm, leg, etc.; whatever is downhill.

leading hand The hand that's further downhill.

length The length of a snowboard (measured in centimeters).

line The route you take on your snowboard; the path from Point A to Point B.

lip The last couple inches of a jump, or the very top of the half-pipe wall.

maneuver zone The section of a feature where you perform a trick; on a jump it's in the air, while on a rail or box it's the place where you are in contact with the rail or box.

nose float The amount of float in snow that's created by the nose of your snowboard.

nose press A rail slide in which you put all your weight on the nose of your board and hold up the tail.

ollie A jump into the air with your snowboard attached to your feet.

packed out Typically refers to boots that have lost their support from overuse.

pillow lines Snow formations that look like pillows.

pop The flex of a board: A new snowboard with a snappy responsive flex is said to have a lot of pop. Also used to describe jumps built with steep angles of trajectory: A jump that sends a rider high in the air has a lot of pop.

poppy Used to describe a jump that has a steep trajectory and will send you high in the air.

pow Light, fluffy snow. Also called *freshies, blower*.

pressing your board Putting all your weight on either the nose or tail of your board and balancing on it.

rails Steel pipes meant for snowboards to slide on.

regular Riding with your left foot forward or leading.

rocker The opposite of camber: A board with rocker rises at the nose and tail.

rollers Large, groomed piles of snow that roll over in a smooth arc.

quarter-pipe Half of a half-pipe.

quiver A large collection of a lot of different kinds of boards.

S-shaped rails Rails that are shaped like the letter S.

scrub To slow down by applying pressure to your edges.

sessioning To hit a feature over and over.

set-up turn A small turn made just before a jump or rail that lets you get comfortable.

shifty A trick in which you jump in the air and rotate the lower half of your body in the opposite direction of your upper half.

shred To ride hard.

sidecut The amount of arc in your edge, which is what allows for smoother turns.

slash To turn your board quickly and aggressively and throw a lot of snow in the air.

speed check A small turn made just before a jump or rail that slows you down.

stance The orientation of your feet on your snowboard.

straight air Jumping without rotating at all.

switch Riding down the hill with the foot that's typically your trailing foot as your leading foot. Also called *fakie*.

tabletop A jump that looks like a pyramid with the top cut off, on which the deck is flat, like a table.

tail float The amount of float in snow that's created by the tail of your snowboard.

tail press (tail wheelie) A rail slide in which you put all your weight on the tail of your board and hold up the nose.

takeoff zone (jump) The part of a feature where you leave the ground.

toe edge The edge of your board that's situated under your toes.

toe strap The strap on your binding that goes over the toebox on your boot.

trailing hand Your uphill hand.

transceiver See *beacon*.

transition (tranny) A section of a slope of snow that's angled, either naturally or man-made.

vert (n), verty (adj) The section of a half-pipe or quarter-pipe wall that is at a vertical or nearly vertical angle to the ground.

waist The mid-section of your board.

wall ride A feature in a terrain park that looks like a wall.

wash out To lose your edge hold and slip out.

wind up To turn your upper body in the opposite direction that you're going to spin.

Index

Page numbers in **bold** refer to illustrations.

About the Author

Liam Gallagher is an associate editor at *TransWorld Snowboarding Magazine*. After graduating from the University of Montana with a degree in journalism, he worked at ski resorts around Montana building and maintaining terrain parks. His writing and photography have appeared in snowboard magazines worldwide including *Snowboarder, Frequency: The Snowboarder's Journal, Method Magazine* and *Australian Snowboarder.* He lives in Cardiff, California.

THE MOUNTAINEERS, founded in 1906, is a nonprofit outdoor activity and conservation club, whose mission is "to explore, study, preserve, and enjoy the natural beauty of the outdoors ...." Based in Seattle, Washington, the club is now one of the largest such organizations in the United States, with seven branches throughout Washington State.

The Mountaineers sponsors both classes and year-round outdoor activities in the Pacific Northwest, which include hiking, mountain climbing, ski-touring, snowshoeing, bicycling, camping, canoeing and kayaking, nature study, sailing, and adventure travel. The club's conservation division supports environmental causes through educational activities, sponsoring legislation, and presenting informational programs.

All club activities are led by skilled, experienced volunteers, who are dedicated to promoting safe and responsible enjoyment and preservation of the outdoors.

If you would like to participate in these organized outdoor activities or the club's programs, consider a membership in The Mountaineers. For information and an application, write or call The Mountaineers, Club Headquarters, 7700 Sand Point Way NE, Seattle, WA 98115; 206-521-6001. You can also visit the club's website at www.mountaineers.org or contact The Mountaineers via email at clubmail@mountaineers.org.

The Mountaineers Books, an active, nonprofit publishing program of the club, produces guidebooks, instructional texts, historical works, natural history guides, and works on environmental conservation. All books produced by The Mountaineers Books fulfill the club's mission. Visit www.mountaineersbooks.org to find details about all our titles and the latest author events, as well as videos, web clips, links, and more!

The Mountaineers Books
1001 SW Klickitat Way, Suite 201
Seattle, WA 98134
800-553-4453
mbooks@mountaineersbooks.org

The Mountaineers Books is proud to be a corporate sponsor of The Leave No Trace Center for Outdoor Ethics, whose mission is to promote and inspire responsible outdoor recreation through education, research, and partnerships. The Leave No Trace program is focused specifically on human-powered (nonmotorized) recreation. Leave No Trace strives to educate visitors about the nature of their recreational impacts, as well as offer techniques to prevent and minimize such impacts. Leave No Trace is best understood as an educational and ethical program, not as a set of rules and regulations.
For more information, visit www.lnt.org, or call 800-332-4100.

OTHER TITLES YOU MIGHT ENJOY FROM THE MOUNTAINEERS BOOKS

The Avalanche Handbook, 3rd Edition
McClung & Schaerer
The unrivaled resource used by the pros for avalanche information and snow conditions

Snowshoeing: From Novice to Master
Prater
From woods to mountains, easy techniques for beginning, intermediate, and experienced snowshoers

100 Classic Backcountry Ski and Snowboard Routes in Washington
Burgdorfer
Classic descents and backcountry routes including maps, access, elevation profiles, and much more

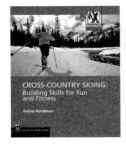

Cross Country Skiing: Building Skills for Fun and Fitness
Hindman
Instruction for novice and intermediate cross-country skiers

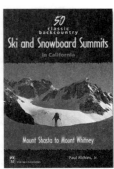

50 Classic Backcountry Ski and Snowboard Summits in California
Richens
Classic descents and backcountry routes in California

Staying Alive in Avalanche Terrain, 2nd edition
Tremper
Accessible and up-to-date manual for outdoor enthusiasts